Contents

Health and safety in motor vehicle repair and associated industries

HSE Books

54050000370478

18th August 2011

First published 2009

ISBN 978 0 7176 6308 8

This guidance is issued by the Health and Safety Executive. Following the guidance is not compulsory and you are free to take other action. But if you do follow the guidance you will normally be doing enough to comply with the law. Health and safety inspectors seek to secure compliance with the law and may refer to this guidance as illustrating good practice.

Introduction

1   This book is aimed at owners, managers and self-employed operators of motor vehicle repair (MVR) businesses and their health and safety advisers. It may also be of interest to employees and safety representatives. The guidance covers:

- vehicle maintenance and repair (including tyre, exhaust and windscreen replacement);
- body repair, refinishing and valeting;
- MOT testing; and
- the roadside recovery of vehicles.

2   Most of these activities are carried out at MVR garages and 'fast-fit' centres, but also at commercial and domestic customers' premises, and at the roadside. MVR businesses increasingly take on a wider range of services, such as air conditioning and glass repair. The industry employs around 170 000 people and is dominated by small and medium-sized businesses. Over half the workforce are in businesses employing fewer than ten people and many are self-employed.

3   Most accidents in MVR involve slips, trips and falls or occur during lifting and handling, and often cause serious injury. Crushing incidents involving the movement or collapse of vehicles under repair result in serious injuries and deaths every year. Petrol-related work is a common cause of serious burns and fires, some fatal.

4   There is also widespread potential for work-related ill health in MVR. Many of the substances used require careful storage, handling and control. Isocyanate-containing paints have been the biggest cause of occupational asthma in the UK for many years and MVR is also in the top ten industries for cases of disabling dermatitis. Use of power tools can cause vibration white finger.

5   This guidance has been developed in consultation with representatives from the MVR industry and describes good practice. Following it should help you reduce the likelihood of accidents or damage to health. The book is divided into two main sections, one has guidance for specific industry sectors and the other provides extensive advice on common MVR issues.

Guidance for specific MVR sectors

Servicing and mechanical repair

6   This is a wide-ranging area and includes routine maintenance and diagnostic work, as well as major mechanical repair. There are a number of health and safety issues to consider, including those set out below.

Used engine oils

7   Frequent and prolonged contact with used engine oil may cause dermatitis and other skin disorders, including skin cancer, so avoid unnecessary contact. Adopt safe systems of work and wear protective clothing (see Figure 1), which should be cleaned or replaced regularly. Maintain high standards of personal hygiene and cleanliness.

8   Encourage employees exposed to used engine oils to carry out self-inspection (see the HSE guidance sheet *Work with lubricants and waste oil*).[1] If you have any doubts, consult a doctor.

Engine running

9   You may need to run engines for diagnostic purposes but exhaust fumes irritate the eyes and respiratory tract, and are a risk to health if you breathe them in. Carbon-fuelled engine fumes contain carbon monoxide, a poisonous gas. Prolonged exposure to diesel fumes, especially blue or black smoke, may lead to coughing and breathlessness. Long-term repeated exposure to diesel fumes over a period of about 20 years may increase the risk of lung cancer.

10   Exhaust fumes can quickly reach harmful concentrations, particularly from cold or intermittently run engines (when run indoors without exhaust ventilation). Provide extraction or exhaust equipment, preferably by direct coupling to the vehicle exhaust (see Figure 2). It should ventilate to a safe place in the open air – where fume will not be drawn back into the workshop or affect other premises or people nearby. This is particularly important when working in a vehicle inspection pit (see paragraph 228). Maintain couplings and flexible connections in good condition to prevent leaks.

Figure 1 Wearing nitrile gloves to reduce hand contamination when draining used engine oils

Figure 2 Exhaust extraction

11 Don't rely on catalytic converters to run engines safely indoors. They are less effective when exhaust gases are relatively cool, eg from vehicles idling for long periods or used intermittently for short periods. Catalytic converters do not remove toxic oxides of nitrogen.

12 See the HSE guidance sheet on *Vehicle exhaust fumes (in warehouses, garages etc)*[2] for further information.

Rolling roads and brake testing

13 Rolling road equipment ranges from relatively slow, two-wheel rotation for brake testing up to high-speed, four-wheel drive installations commonly used for engine testing and tuning. Rolling road brake-testing equipment is typically installed in the workshop floor as part of an MOT test station, while high-speed facilities are usually in dedicated rooms (see Figure 3).

14 Serious injuries have been caused by operators trying to make adjustments or repairs to vehicles on rolling roads. Restrict use of all rolling roads to trained and competent operators and prevent unauthorised access to areas where testing is carried out.

15 It is important to take precautions when working with this type of equipment:

■ Fit hold-to-run controls for brake-testing equipment (and ensure they work).
■ Fit guards at the sides of rollers where access can't be prevented.
■ When it is not in use, isolate brake-testing equipment from the mains and place cover plates over the rollers.

■ Maintain the grip of the running surfaces of the brake tester to reduce the need to dry tyres and test surfaces. Do not try to dry them while they are in motion or carry out other testing or adjustments on the vehicle while the rolling road is moving.
■ Where brake-testing equipment is sited over a pit, people should be prevented from entering the pit while a test is running.

16 Some manufacturers have developed rolling brake-testing equipment (where the road wheels typically run at less than 5 km/h) that will also perform high-speed operations such as tachograph calibration (typically over 50 km/h). Before installing such dual-purpose equipment into existing rolling brake-testing installations, do an assessment to identify additional precautions for protecting against risks from high-speed running, such as:

■ protecting against material being ejected from tyres;
■ segregation of the area and preventing access to people in the vicinity;
■ entry and exit routes of vehicles under test;
■ exposure to noise and exhaust emissions.

17 Rolling road and brake-testing equipment should be inspected under regulation 6 of the Provision and Use of Work Equipment Regulations (PUWER),[3] typically every year.

Figure 3 Rolling road

Figure 4 Brake-cleaning equipment

Brake and clutch servicing

18 The use of asbestos in vehicle brake, clutch and gasket components was prohibited from 1999, with the exception that pre-1973 vehicles could continue to be fitted with asbestos-containing brake shoes until the end of 2004. So it is possible that some old vehicles could contain asbestos and sensible precautions should be taken. But remember that all brake and clutch dust is potentially harmful so:

■ never blow dust out of brake drums or clutch housings with an airline;
■ use properly designed brake-cleaning equipment which prevents dust escaping (see Figure 4); or
■ use clean, wet rags to clean out drums or housings and dispose of used rags in a plastic waste bag while still wet.

If you do need to dispose of asbestos waste, follow the guidance in HSE's Asbestos essentials sheet EM9 *Disposal of asbestos waste*.[4]

Vehicle valeting

19 Valeting may be carried out as a separate operation or as incidental to other work, such as routine vehicle servicing. Many proprietary cleaners are relatively harmless, but others can contain toxic or flammable solvents and prolonged skin contact with cleaners and detergents can cause dermatitis. Direct skin and eye contact with such substances can also be harmful (see the product label and hazard data sheet). Assess the hazards and risks involved and use products that create the least risk.

20 Remember that substances that are safe to use in a well-ventilated workshop may not be safe in an enclosed vehicle.

21 Use working methods that minimise the amount of solvent used, eg pour only small amounts of fluid onto a pad or applicator from a small container, which is kept closed when not in use.

22 For adequate ventilation during valeting:

■ make sure the working area is well ventilated;
■ when working inside vehicles, leave all doors and sunroofs wide open; and
■ assess whether forced ventilation (eg a fan) is required to blow fresh air through the vehicle to dilute any solvent vapours.

23 Never use aerosols or solvent-based trigger sprayers near a naked flame.

24 Wear protective clothing, including eye protection and suitable gloves such as single-use nitrile gloves. If you must use latex gloves, make sure they are 'low-protein, powder-free'. Always throw away single-use gloves when you take them off.

25 Choose an application method that reduces the risk of clothing contamination, but if contamination does occur, remove and dry the clothing in a safe place in the open air.

Airbags and seat belt pretensioners

26 Most modern vehicles have airbags and seat belt pretensioners and these may need repair or replacement over time. Many devices use an explosive charge and, if they are accidently discharged, there is the possibility of physical injury or exposure to harmful substances. Anyone carrying out work on them therefore needs to be aware of the risks and the precautions to take.

27 Find out the UN hazard classification of the airbags and seat belt pretensioners you store and handle, and the net explosive quantity of the devices from your supplier. If UN Hazard Class 1 (explosive) devices are kept and the combined total of explosive exceeds 5 kg (typically about 50 devices), the premises need to be licensed and registered with the local authority. If the quantity is 5 kg or below, the following precautions will still be appropriate.

28 Premises storing UN Hazard Class 2 or UN Hazard Class 9 devices do not need to be registered, but the devices should be kept under similar conditions to Class 1 devices.

Storing airbags and seat belt pretensioners
29 Always store airbags and seat belt pretensioners in suitable containers. To meet the requirements for registration, containers need to:

■ be substantial;
■ have no exposed steel;
■ be easy to keep clean; and
■ be closable and lockable.

30 Keep the container away from:

■ oils, paints and other flammable material;
■ areas where hot work, such as welding or brazing, takes place; and
■ electricity cables, sockets, distribution boards etc.

31 Also make sure the container is:

■ secured to the wall or floor if possible; and
■ kept dry at all times.

Handling airbags and seat belt pretensioners

32 Always check the manufacturer's or supplier's information before starting work on vehicles containing airbags and pretensioners, as procedural differences will occur from make to make.

33 Never place your head or body close to the front of an undischarged device, especially when fitting it, or removing it from a vehicle. Carry the module with the trim cover facing away from you. Do not place a module, or steering wheel assembly fitted with an airbag, face (trim-side) down or with the trim against a hard surface. Never attempt to repair or modify devices.

34 If work is required on an airbag module, such as testing, it should be mounted securely on a bench or jig to allow enough space for the bag to inflate freely if it is triggered accidentally (see Figure 5).

35 Never expose airbag modules to excessive heat (over 90 ºC), impact, electrical current (including static electricity) or radio transmitters.

36 Always use new components. Return any modules that are damaged or appear suspect to your supplier, except where the damage has caused the contents of the inflator cartridge to be exposed or spilt, in which case get specialist advice from your supplier.

37 Return undischarged devices to your supplier, using the packaging it was supplied in. If the packaging is unavailable, contact your supplier and ask them to provide it.

38 Devices should only be discharged by appropriately trained personnel, working to the manufacturer's procedures.

39 Get advice from your supplier before disposing of any discharged devices. Some manufacturers advise that their discharged airbags or seat belt pretensioners can be disposed of, or recycled, as normal waste; others recommend that they are treated as hazardous waste.

40 It is illegal to dispose of explosives as normal waste and domestic/commercial waste bins must not be used for disposing of undischarged airbags or seat belt pretensioners in Class 1.

41 The HSE leaflet *A guide to handling and storage of airbags and seat belt pretensioners at garages and motor vehicle repair shops*[5] gives comprehensive guidance for those handling, storing or transporting larger numbers of these devices.

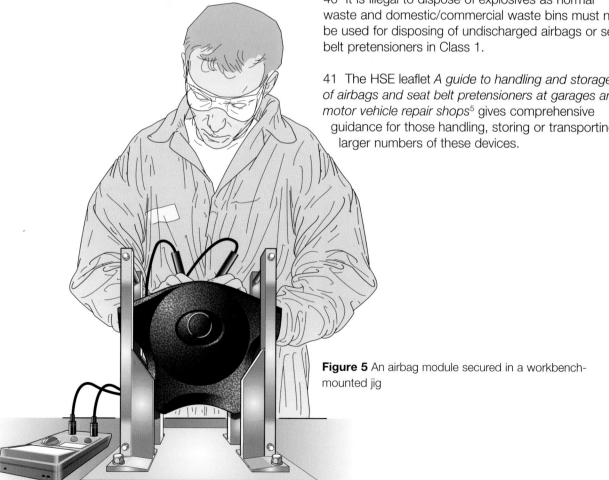

Figure 5 An airbag module secured in a workbench-mounted jig

Air-conditioning systems

42 Most modern vehicles are fitted with air-conditioning units, using hydrofluorocarbons ('F-gases') as refrigerants. 'Freon' (R12) was banned due to environmental concerns and all new vehicles from 1995 have used tetrafluoroethane (R134a). R12 should not be used to maintain older systems.

43 Draining and replenishing of refrigerant is usually carried out using a recharging unit (see Figure 6). The main risks to health and safety associated with refrigerants used in air-conditioning systems occur if they are released into the atmosphere. Table 1 has advice on reducing these risks, which include:

■ frostbite, caused by skin or eye contact with the refrigerant liquid or gas;
■ asphyxiation, if the gas (which is heavier than air) escapes into a vehicle inspection pit or similar confined space; and
■ toxic and corrosive gases, resulting from thermal decomposition of refrigerant if exposed to temperatures above 250 °C.

44 There is also a risk of explosion if hot work, such as welding or burning, is carried out on or near air-conditioning systems. This arises because:

■ high temperatures could cause the system pressure to increase significantly; and
■ although R134a is not flammable at normal temperature and pressure, it can become combustible when mixed with air under pressure and exposed to strong ignition sources.

Figure 6 Air-conditioning recharging unit

Bodyshops and SMART spraying

45 This sector of the industry carries out repairs to vehicle bodywork and components and respraying. Work may include removal and replacement of panels, bumpers and damaged parts, vehicle straightening, dent removal, body filling and preparation before painting. Developments in car manufacturing lead to changes in repair techniques and, potentially, exposure to new workplace hazards.

46 Small and Medium Area Repair Technique ('SMART') work involves 'cosmetic' repair to a variety of vehicle components. It is often carried out off-site where exposure to hazardous substances may be harder to control. The size of the job means the quantity of chemicals used is significantly less than for conventional repairs, but there is still potential for harm, particularly from paint spraying.

Body filling and preparation

47 The Control of Substances Hazardous to Health Regulations 2002 (COSHH)[6] have a strategy for the assessment and control of the hazards involved in body filling and preparation, which you should adopt. Firstly, use less harmful materials, but if this is not reasonably practicable:

■ use exhaust ventilation to control exposure to substances you need to use; and
■ use personal protective equipment (PPE) as a last resort.

48 Most fillers used in MVR consist of a thermosetting unsaturated polyester in a solvent which is mixed with a reactive hardener. Styrene or methacrylates are often in these mixtures, and they have powerful odours. Hardeners are usually skin irritants and some are strong skin sensitisers – both can cause dermatitis. Similarly, glass fibre fillers can irritate skin (see paragraphs 397-407 for advice on skin care).

49 Powered disc cutting and sanding of any bodywork fillers creates large quantities of dust, invisible under normal lighting. Even if the dust does not contain specific harmful substances, the quantity generated can be damaging to health.

Table 1 Controlling the risks from air-conditioning systems

DO	DON'T
Follow the instructions of the air-conditioning system's manufacturer and the refrigerant supplier, and any other relevant advice[7]	Don't work on or near an air-conditioning system unless the risks and precautions to be taken have been identified
Identify the refrigerant in the system before carrying out any work	Don't assume that the system is free from refrigerant gases until this has been proved (for example with a system pressure gauge), particularly where the vehicle has been involved in an accident
Use approved equipment when maintaining or servicing the system	Don't overfill refrigerant containers
Ensure that everyone using the equipment or working on the system has been properly trained and is adequately supervised. Under environmental legislation, MVR servicing of air-conditioning units containing 'F-gases' such as R12 and R134a can only be carried out by appropriately qualified staff	Don't mix refrigerants R12 and R134a when recharging the system. Check with manufacturers before blending alternative chemicals
Store containers of refrigerant chemicals in a safe place away from direct heat	Don't deliberately discharge F-gases into the atmosphere
Wear appropriate eye protection, gloves and other protective equipment when handling the refrigerant or working on the system to protect against the effects of refrigerant liquid or gas	Don't carry out any work on a system containing F-gases over or close to a vehicle inspection pit or similar confined space as people working there could suffocate
Train staff in the emergency actions to be taken in the case of spillage of liquid or release of gas	Don't allow smoking, welding, burning or other hot work in areas where F-gases may be present as this could produce harmful breakdown products
Find out from vehicle manufacturers whether refrigerant should be removed from the system before you carry out refinishing/respraying work in a spraybake oven	Don't carry out welding, soldering, burning or other hot work on or near air-conditioning systems as this could raise the pressure inside the system and cause an explosion
Make adequate arrangements for the safe recovery and disposal of old or waste refrigerant, including any contained in scrap receptacles or equipment	Don't carry out any roadside work on vehicles involved in accidents until the air-conditioning system has been checked for possible leaks or other damage
Check that all the refrigerant has been recovered before removing the air-conditioning system from a vehicle to be scrapped or recycled	Don't attempt roadside repairs to air-conditioning systems unless trained mechanics and approved equipment are available

50 Lead has historically been used in some body preparation operations. Although the temperature at which the alloy is applied is usually not high enough to generate large quantities of harmful fume, subsequent finishing by powered disc cutting and sanding can release high concentrations of fine dust, which is a serious health hazard.

51 For all body preparation work:

■ Minimise the number of people exposed to dust and fume.
■ Keep dust to a minimum. Large excesses of filler can be removed using coarse hand files. For powered disc cutting and sanding, use tools with built-in dust extraction (see Figures 7, 8 and 9), or use local exhaust ventilation such as an extracted booth.
■ Where necessary, use personal protective equipment (PPE): Type FFP2 respiratory protection may be required, dependent on the efficiency of the extraction system. Type 5 (BS EN ISO 13982-1) disposable overalls help prevent dust accumulating on clothing.
■ Provide separate changing areas for clean and contaminated clothing (see paragraph 409).

Storing and mixing paints

52 Many paints and solvents used in vehicle finishing give off flammable vapour, which is hazardous to health if breathed in. The escape of solvent vapours should be kept to a minimum.

53 Designate a suitably fire-resisting room for paint mixing and ensure there is adequate ventilation to prevent build-up of flammable vapours (eg more than five air changes per hour). It may be beneficial to connect the room ventilation to the lighting circuit and incorporate a timed extraction overrun. Under these circumstances, respiratory protective equipment (RPE) should not be necessary, even when mixing isocyanate paints.

Figure 7 Powered sanding with normal lighting and no extraction – very little dust is visible

Figure 8 Powered sanding with no extraction – special lighting shows up the dust generated

Figure 9 Powered sanding with special lighting shows the effectiveness of extraction

54 When not in use, flammable liquid containers should be kept closed and stored in suitable fire-resistant cabinets or bins, designed to retain spills (110 per cent of the largest container normally stored). The maximum quantities for cabinet or bin storage are:

- no more than 50 litres for extremely or highly flammable products and flammable liquids with a flashpoint below the maximum ambient temperature of the workroom/working area; and
- no more than 250 litres for other flammable liquids with a higher flashpoint, up to 55 °C.

55 Keep larger stocks in a secure, open-air storage area or in a separate fire-resisting store with spillage retention and good ventilation.

56 Proprietary paint-mixing systems reduce the quantities of paints stored and minimise vapour given off during mixing. Exclude sources of ignition and ensure that all electrical equipment around potential flammable sources (eg the mixer) is correctly Ex-rated (see paragraphs 266-283 for further details).

57 Keep lids on cans and keep containers closed to stop vapour escaping. Contain spillages by decanting paint over a tray and have absorbent material readily available to soak up spillages. Keep contaminated material in a lidded metal bin, and dispose of its contents safely.

58 Treat empty flammable liquid containers in the same way as full ones unless they have been properly inerted – they will often be full of vapour.

59 Avoid skin contact by using single-use nitrile gloves or similar.

60 Spills of reactive hardeners and empty hardener containers need decontamination before disposal. Check for decontaminant information in the product's safety data sheet, or ask the product maker for advice.

Paint spraying with isocyanate paints

61 Most vehicle paints are cured using isocyanate hardeners. The precautions outlined below provide health protection against isocyanate-containing paints. Using the same precautions provides protection against most other paint types.

62 Almost all MVR bodyshops use isocyanate-containing paints. Isocyanates are used in some water-based paints and almost all lacquers. Remember that **water-based does not mean isocyanate-free**.

63 Breathing in isocyanate paint mist can cause asthma and vehicle paint sprayers are 80 times more likely to get this disease than the general worker. Many people mistakenly believe isocyanates in vehicle paints cause cancer or contain cyanide and are poisonous – they don't.

64 Early signs of respiratory sensitisation to isocyanates include one or more of the following:

- chest tightness – often occurring outside working hours in the evening or early morning;
- persistent cough;
- wheezing;
- breathlessness; and
- flu-like shivers.

65 If a person has early symptoms and their isocyanate exposure continues, they may suffer from permanent and severe asthma. There is no cure and at this stage asthma can be triggered by everyday smells or even cold air. Being this disabled has life-changing consequences and even a tiny amount of any isocyanate could trigger an attack. It would almost certainly mean the person has to give up their current job.

66 The risk is completely preventable, but it requires:

- proper design, application and use of spray booths and rooms;
- following correct working procedures;
- using air-fed breathing apparatus;
- checking that the controls are working properly;
- carrying out health checks on those likely to be exposed to isocyanate paint mist.

Proper design, application and use of spray booths and rooms

67 The main source of isocyanate exposure is paint spraying. Exposure may also occur from cleaning the spray gun and low exposures may occur from baking. Exposure from dry sanding of fresh isocyanate paint film, rollering isocyanate-containing paints and skin or eye contact with paint mist is so small as to be undetectable.

68 Paint leaves a spray gun around 100 metres/ second. This creates a fan of visible paint and large quantities of paint mist that is invisible under normal lighting. This invisible mist behaves like smoke, spreading throughout the spray enclosure, enveloping the operator, soon after spraying has started. Special lighting can show up this mist (see Figures 10 and 11).

69 In most spray booths the ventilation causes the air to move at less than 0.5 metres per second (in spray rooms it is even slower). This is overwhelmed by the spray gun air jet, moving around 200 times faster, and having a 'throw' of over 5 metres (see Figure 12). Booth ventilation cannot, as is often imagined, instantly sweep away the airborne paint overspray.

70 It is good practice to use high-volume, low-pressure (HVLP) or 'compliant' paint guns, which produce around half the amount of mist created by a 'traditional' spray gun (provided that the manufacturer's recommendations for air pressure are not exceeded).

71 The more effective the spray booth or room extraction, the lower will be the overall concentration of isocyanate in the air of the enclosure. Even so, isocyanate concentrations in spray rooms can be up

Figure 10 'Now you see it…'. Special lighting and black background show paint mist enveloping the sprayer

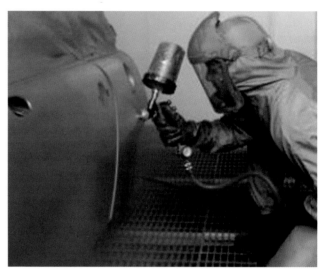

Figure 11 'Now you don't'. Under normal booth lighting the mist is invisible

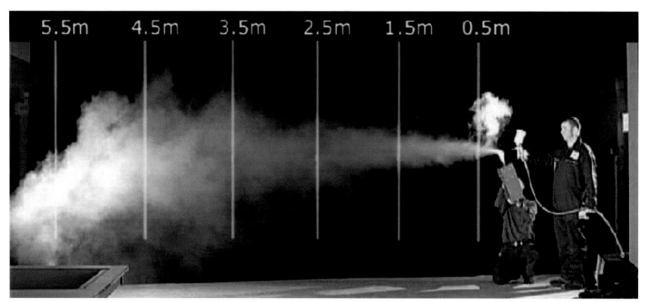

5.5m 4.5m 3.5m 2.5m 1.5m 0.5m

Figure 12 Smoke showing the 'throw' of a spray gun

to 300 times the workplace exposure limit (WEL) and spray booths can be up to 30 times the WEL.

72 Spray rooms are relatively inefficient compared with properly designed spray booths. However, spray rooms are acceptable provided that:

■ mist does not leak out of the room;
■ the extracted air is effectively filtered and discharged safely (eg above roof level);
■ suitable precautions are taken after spraying until the room has cleared of mist. This can take a long time. During this clearance time, the sprayed object must stay in the room and anyone in the room must use air-fed breathing apparatus;
■ arrangements are made so that the sprayer can leave and enter the room safely during the clearance time;
■ evidence from urine tests (biological monitoring) shows that exposure is being adequately controlled.

Measure and know the clearance time of your spray booth or room

73 Once spraying stops, the paint mist is diluted and displaced by the extract air and eventually removed. The time taken for mist removal is known as the 'clearance time' and will vary, depending on the design and air movement. Typically, a booth clears in less than five minutes but a room can take 20 minutes or more.

74 Smoke testing is a practical way to measure the clearance time. 'Party fog' machines are inexpensive and many are suitable for determining clearance times.

See the research report *Review of commercially available party fog machines suitable for determining the clearance time of paint spray booths and rooms.*[8]

75 The boxed text after paragraph 79 sets out the spray booth/room clearance time and leakage test.

76 Large (eg commercial vehicle) booths require a professional smoke generator for clearance testing. A number of organisations offer this service.

77 Clearance times vary. The worst case is likely to be just before you change the extract filters in the booth or room. Initially, test regularly to check the variation in clearance time. Once you have established the likely worst case, you can reduce the frequency of tests. Clearance tests should also form part of the 14-monthly thorough examination and test.

78 Put up a sign at all entrances to the booth or room, similar to Figure 14, that states:

■ the clearance time (in large letters);
■ when it was tested;
■ who did the test;
■ when the next test is due.

79 Automatic clearance time indicators (activated when the spray gun finishes spraying) show when the clearance time has elapsed and the booth is safe to enter without breathing apparatus.

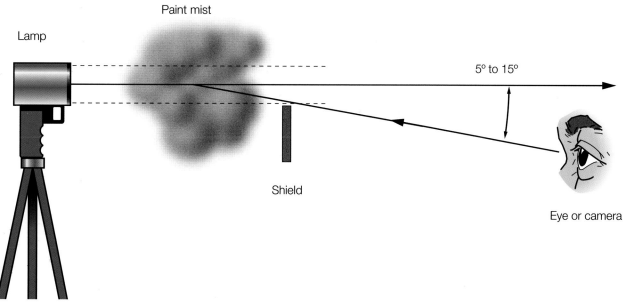

Figure 13 Using a powerful parallel beam torch to show up paint mist

Spray booth/room clearance time and leakage test

- You need to know the clearance time of your spray booth or room.
- Check this just before changing the extract filters to give a 'worst-case' time.
- Include the clearance time test in the 14-monthly 'thorough examination and test', as required by regulation 9 of COSHH.[6] Note that you may need to test more often than this.

Equipment
Fog or smoke machine, an extension lead (for mains-powered machines), a stopwatch or similar, a high 'candle-power' torch on a stand or tripod.

Procedure
- Measure the clearance time with the spray booth or room empty, to avoid greasy deposits on vehicles or body parts.
- Do the test at the normal spraying temperature. Turn the lights on full to help show up the smoke.
- During smoke tests, arrange for someone else to check for any smoke leaks outside the booth/room, or from the ductwork.
- **Pre-test:** Turn the extraction off. Fill the booth/room with smoke. Turn the extraction on, and watch how the smoke clears. Some areas will take longer to clear. Then turn the extraction off again.
- **Test:** Position the torch to shine through the area that clears slowest. Fill the booth/room evenly with smoke. You may need the extension lead to do this properly.
- When you cannot see across the booth/room, it is full of smoke. If the fog machine cuts out, give it time to reheat once or twice to get the right smoke density.
- Turn on the extraction and start the timer. Look towards the torch, 'up' the light beam (see Figure 13).
- The room is clear when you can see no smoke anywhere in the booth/room – especially those areas identified in the pre-test.
- Round up the measured time to the next quarter minute.
- Display this time on a large, clear notice on the entrances to the booth or room. Tell everyone who needs to know.

Things to consider before carrying out a smoke test

Warn people: Warn your employees, and possibly your neighbours, about the smoke test so that they are not alarmed. It may also be necessary to warn the local fire service to avoid unnecessary call-outs.

Precision in clearance time measurement: The clearance time test is imprecise, relying on individual perception of when the booth/room is 'full' of smoke, and when all the smoke has gone. The method is fairly crude but it is good enough to give users the information they need to work safely. Using a high-powered torch to help estimate clearance can increase the measured time by about half a minute. If the booth fans take an appreciable time to run up to normal speed, you may need to make some allowance for clearance time during normal booth working.

Respiratory protection may be needed: The smoke has low toxicity, but if you have a pre-existing lung condition and/or do tests regularly (eg every day) and/or experience discomfort using smoke, wear appropriate RPE. A well-fitting respirator with a combination A/P3 filter will be adequate.

THE CLEARANCE TIME OF THIS SPRAY BOOTH IS:

.... Minutes   .... Seconds

DO NOT raise visor while spraying or during the clearance time

DO NOT enter without air-fed breathing apparatus during the clearance time

ISOCYANATES IN PAINT CAN CAUSE ASTHMA

Test date ....   Spray booth model ....

Test carried out by ....   Spray booth number ....

Date of next test ....

Figure 14 Example of a clearance time poster

'Negative pressure' indicators

80 To prevent paint mist escaping into the workplace, all spray booths and rooms must run at a slightly lower air pressure than the surroundings, so that air only leaks inwards. This is known as running at 'negative pressure' and is required by environmental legislation. All spray booths and rooms require an indicator to show that negative pressure is being maintained.

81 A manometer (or something similar) should be fitted to booths (see Figure 15). For spray rooms something less exact, such as a swinging vane, should be enough (see Figure 16). Check the negative pressure indicator daily to show that the booth or room is working correctly. A clearance smoke test will also show whether the booth or ductwork is leaking.

Commercial vehicle (CV) and other large spray booths

82 These booths can be many times larger than a car booth, but the control principles are similar. Particular issues relating to CV-type booths are outlined below.

83 The smoke test of booth integrity and the clearance time will require a commercial-grade smoke machine. It is possible to become disorientated in large, smoke-filled booths, so the person carrying out the smoke test should fill the booth with smoke, working back to a position near a door and against a wall.

84 Large vehicles can alter the flow patterns, leading to shorter or longer clearance times. So it is good practice to measure the clearance time with and without a vehicle in the booth. Take the 'clearance time' as the longer time.

85 Larger vehicles need longer spraying times, and are likely to create more paint overspray, which can be deposited on the air-fed mask. This will need removing regularly to ensure the sprayer can see the quality of the finish without lifting their visor. Tear-off visor protectors may be helpful.

86 Some large booths have pits in the floor to spray the underside of vehicles. This can create a 'dead space' where mist can linger after the main booth has cleared. It is also possible that flammable concentrations of solvent vapour could accumulate in the pit. Booths should be constructed to minimise this and supplementary measures, such as extraction or air blowers, may be needed.

87 Check the effectiveness of extracted pits by smoke testing. If there is floor extraction but no pit extraction it may be possible to extract the pit through its side. This would be a major alteration and the booth would require recommissioning. Alternatively, use an air mover to blow mist and vapour out of the pit. This is a minor alteration, but you need to check the effect on airflows in the booth (using a smoke test) and the adequacy of breathing apparatus.

88 Working in or near pits requires precautions similar to those outlined in paragraphs 214-232.

89 Spraying commercial vehicles, trailers, buses etc often involves working at height (see Figure 17). Precautions are outlined in paragraphs 368-378.

Figure 15 Example of a manometer fitted to a spray booth

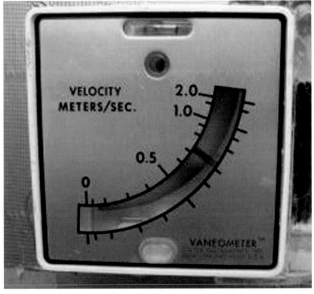

Figure 16 Example of a swinging vane fitted to a spray room

Following correct working procedures

90 Never spray isocyanate-containing paints in an occupied workshop or spray without air-fed breathing apparatus (BA). Even very small jobs (such as SMART repairs) will create high-exposure peaks.

91 Air-fed BA is required for anyone present in the booth or room during spraying, and throughout the clearance time. Many sprayers lift their visor soon after spraying to check the work quality, not knowing they are still surrounded by invisible paint mist. This can cause significant exposure and eliminating the practice is vital to achieve effective control.

92 To leave a booth or room safely during the clearance time:

- walk to the pedestrian door wearing air-fed BA. The air hose must be long enough, and the connection point must be by the door;
- open the door, unplug the airline and put the disconnected hose on a hanger next to the door;
- step out, shut the door and remove the air-fed BA.

93 When gun cleaning, spray-to-dry in the booth or room wearing air-fed BA. Gun-cleaning machines that create mist need extraction because the residues can contain isocyanate.

Using air-fed breathing apparatus (BA)

94 Using air-fed BA is mandatory when spraying isocyanate-based products (see Figure 18). Isocyanate paint mist is tasteless and odourless and filtering face masks can fail to protect without warning. Ideally, you should use visor-type, air-fed BA (certified to BS EN 1835:2000). It should be Class LDH3 and include a low-flow indicator (which may be visual or audible). Visibility through the full-face mask can be improved by using tear-off visor protectors and by ensuring adequate levels of lighting.

95 Half-mask BA (with constant airflow supply) conforming to BS EN 139:1995, or to Class LDM 2 of BS EN 12419:1999, has also proved to be effective and does not need to be removed to see the quality of the work. Half-mask BA should be face-fit tested. You may also find it beneficial to have a separate visor or goggles, to protect against paint splashes.

96 All BA users should be trained in wearing it, looking after it and testing that it works properly every time.

97 The breathing air supplied to the BA should be uncontaminated and in a quantity sufficient to provide adequate protection of the user. The manufacturer's instruction manual for visor-type devices should specify 'minimum flow conditions' in terms of tubing length and internal bore and air pressure. The standards for

Figure 17 A spray booth for commercial vehicles with moveable gantries provides safe access for spraying at height

half-mask, air-fed devices specify a minimum airflow rate of 120 l/min and, if adjustable, a maximum airflow rate of at least 300 l/min. The low-flow warning device (see paragraph 94) should be designed so that it immediately lets the wearer know if the apparatus is not supplying the manufacturer's minimum design flow rate.

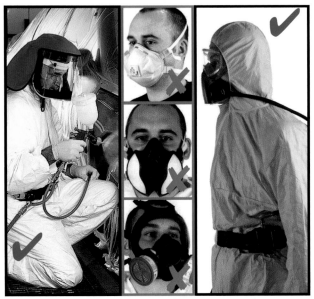

Figure 18 Use only air-fed breathing apparatus when spraying isocyanate paints

98 The COSHH Approved Code of Practice[6] suggests that air supplied to BA should be tested at least every three months to make sure it meets the standards laid out in BS 4275:1997. It may be possible to collect supporting information (eg previous air quality test results and comprehensive maintenance logs) that would provide enough confidence in air quality to extend the period of inspection to six months or, at most, yearly.

Checking that the controls are working properly

99 Ensure that COSHH control measures such as plant or equipment (including engineering controls and PPE) are maintained in an efficient state, in efficient working order, in good repair and in a clean condition (COSHH regulation 9), and suitable records are kept for at least five years.

100 In addition to regular maintenance and checks, spray booths and rooms require a statutory 'thorough examination and test' by a competent person at least once every 14 months. This should include air velocity movements and smoke tests for clearance and leakage. The examiner should attach a label to the spray booth or room stating when it was tested and examined, by whom, and when it should be re-tested. If the booth or room fails the examination and test (eg paint mist leaks from the enclosure), the examiner should attach a red label stating the fault.

101 Train someone to examine all air-fed BA once a month, in accordance with the manufacturer's recommendations. Again, keep suitable records.

Biological monitoring
102 Control of exposure to isocyanate in paint mist requires a combination of measures including:

■ using the right spray gun;
■ containment and extraction of paint mist;
■ use of air-fed BA with a clean air supply;
■ keeping the visor in place during the clearance time etc.

103 Employers have a legal duty to ensure adequate control. But protection requires the continued effectiveness of this combination of mechanical provisions (which can deteriorate) and operator behaviour (which can be inconsistent). Biological monitoring checks the effectiveness of all the protective measures in one go, by measuring diamine (converted from isocyanate in the body) in the sprayer's urine. Evidence from MVR bodyshops shows that when controls work correctly, exposure is prevented and measurements cannot detect any diamine.

104 Biological monitoring has some limitations:

■ Diamine is washed out of the body within hours so it is important to collect the urine sample straight after spraying has finished. Biological monitoring indicates whether exposure to isocyanates occurred. The organisation responsible for managing the tests should explain the results, so you can take remedial action, if necessary.
■ Diamine in urine does not tell you how someone was exposed – only that exposure occurred. In most cases, you should be able to spot what is going wrong and improve control measures. Take repeat samples after making changes to show the results are 'clear'.

105 COSHH requires monitoring of exposure when there is a suitable procedure, and it is not obvious from another method of evaluation that exposure is being adequately controlled. Biological monitoring provides a suitable procedure and is currently the most practical method of monitoring control of personal exposure from isocyanate spraying. Biological monitoring is **not** health surveillance.

106 Carry out biological monitoring during the first few months of employment to show that RPE and working practices are sufficient to control isocyanate exposure. It is good practice thereafter to have urine samples for spray painters monitored once a year, and more often if you use half-mask air-fed BA in spray rooms. Further information on biological monitoring can be found in *Biological monitoring in the workplace*,[9] and in COSHH essentials sheet *Urine sampling for isocyanate exposure measurement*.[10]

Health surveillance
107 Given the historically large numbers of bodyshop workers who have developed asthma, 'high-level' health surveillance has been required (under COSHH regulation 11) for all those potentially exposed – usually the paint sprayers. It should be provided by a competent person, for instance an occupational health nurse or a medical practitioner or other suitable provider familiar with the risks of working with isocyanates and experienced in assessing early signs of occupational asthma.

108 Normally, health surveillance includes annual lung function testing by spirometry and a questionnaire. For new employees it should be carried out on beginning work that may cause exposure: after six weeks; 12 weeks; and then annually. See COSHH essentials sheet *Health surveillance for occupational asthma*.[11] If a bodyshop is well managed and can show (for example by biological monitoring) that isocyanate exposure is consistently well controlled, then 'low-level' respiratory health surveillance (eg using questionnaires) may be all that is required.

109 Health surveillance (skin checks) for dermatitis will normally be appropriate for body preparation workers and paint sprayers (see paragraphs 397-407).

Small and Medium Area Repair Technique (SMART)

110 'SMART' work involves repairs to minor vehicle damage such as dents, chips, scratches and tears to the panels, bumpers, wheel arches, alloy wheels, interior trim and windscreens. Many substances used are hazardous but the small quantities and application methods mean that simple precautions, such as avoiding skin contact and ensuring adequate ventilation (fresh air), are normally sufficient. However, paint spraying is more hazardous and guidance on the necessary precautions is given below.

111 SMART spraying means spray application of a surface coating to parts of motor vehicles, usually outside a spray booth or spray room. The parts coated, as part of a repair, should not normally extend to a complete panel or panels.

112 Typically, spraying is either with a mini-jet spray gun (see Figure 19) or airbrush, eg inlet pressure up to 2 bar, an airflow less than 150 l/min and fluid flow below 100 g/min, or a pre-packaged aerosol spray can.

Figure 19 SMART spraying with a mini-jet gun

113 Paints dry naturally by solvent evaporation or cure by UV light, chemical hardener, or other means. The quantity of paint sprayed is unlikely to exceed 25 ml per coat and spray time is unlikely to exceed one minute per coat, though the spray job may take a few minutes.

114 SMART spraying coatings can be classified as 'reactive' or 'conventional'. Reactive coatings include one-pack products and two-pack products that require mixing before use. They can be solvent-based or water-based.

115 Many products are flammable or highly flammable and need safe storage. The small quantities used in SMART spraying mean that any fire risk during application is likely to lie within 15 cm of the sprayer nozzle.

116 The health hazards depend on the chemistry, but for **reactive products**:

- isocyanate-based products may cause asthma and dermatitis. This includes water-based products that contain isocyanates;
- UV-curable products may cause dermatitis, and may contain isocyanate;
- other products (eg acid-cured) may cause symptoms at least as serious as solvent-based products, eg eye, nose and throat irritation, and mild, reversible effects on the body.

117 The health hazards of solvent-based **conventional spraying products** (commonly known as 'cellulose paints') include irritation of the eyes, nose and throat, and mild, reversible effects on the body.

Personal protective equipment

118 All SMART spraying with reactive products requires respiratory and skin protection.

119 Filtering facepiece respirators are not suitable for users of **isocyanate-based products**. They should preferably use air-fed BA (see paragraphs 94-97) with an assigned protection factor (APF) of 20 or higher, that is:

- LDM2 air-fed half-mask; or
- LDH3 air-fed visor.

120 The compressor must deliver enough clean air for the respirator to work properly. Prevent contamination of the breathing air supply by keeping the compressor and its air intake upwind or outside the spray area and clear of other harmful substances. If you cannot reliably achieve enough compressor capacity, it may be possible to use suitable powered respirators.

121 It is good practice to use the same types of PPE for spraying **non-reactive products** (see Figure 20). However, half-mask filtering facepieces with an APF of 10 or higher can be used, and disposable RPE is acceptable.

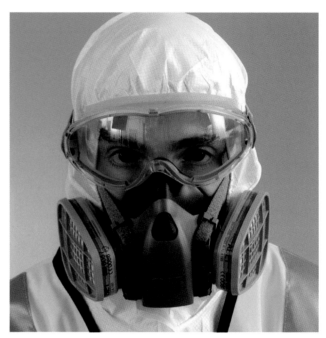

Figure 20 Filtering facepiece RPE for non-reactive products

122 Check that there is a good flow of clean air to the respirator every time it is used. Air-fed RPE should have low-flow alarms.

123 At least once a week, check that the compressor and airlines are in good condition and that the filters and traps are clean. Record these checks in a logbook with details of any part replacements (eg exhalation valves for half-mask respirators, face seals for visors).

124 The relevant British Standard (BS 4275:1997) proposes three-month checks of the airflow and air quality. With good records, and confidence in the air quality, you may only need to check the airflow and air quality once or twice a year (see paragraph 98).

125 Many product mists are irritating to the eyes. If you use a half-mask respirator, you may also need chemical protective goggles.

126 Use overalls of any material, with a hood and nitrile single-use gloves. Single-use gloves are disposable – throw them away after each spray application.

Exposure checks and health surveillance

127 Sprayers using **isocyanate-based products** need to check that the controls are working by carrying out biological monitoring (see paragraphs 102-106). Health surveillance is needed to detect the onset of asthma and skin disease (see paragraphs 107-109).

Spray location

128 You need to prevent unprotected people being exposed to spray. Exclude unprotected bystanders and customers.

Spraying indoors

129 SMART spraying in a spray booth or room should follow the guidance in paragraphs 67-89.

130 It may be possible to spray in the workshop if using a receiving hood extraction system to contain and remove overspray and mist. Check they work effectively using a smoke ('party fog') machine as described in paragraph 74.

Spraying outdoors

131 Keep everyone without air-fed RPE a minimum of 5 metres (but preferably 10 metres) away from spraying. At this distance the health risk is minimal (see Figure 21).

132 Wear all PPE for gun priming, spraying and gun cleaning. Keep wearing your RPE until the job – and gun cleaning – has ended. Ensure the compressor and its air intake are upwind of spraying and clear of other harmful substances.

Decontamination

133 Decontaminate spills of reactive hardeners and empty hardener containers before disposal. Check for decontaminant recipes in the product's safety data sheet, or ask the product maker for advice.

Further information on SMART spraying

134 Further details are given in the free publication *Motor vehicle repair: Good practice for SMART sprayers.*[12]

Figure 21 Coning off an area for spraying outdoors

Tyre and wheel removal, replacement and repair

135 Tyre repair and replacement exposes people to a variety of hazards in addition to those related to movement and lifting of vehicles. Increasing size, weight and pressure, as well as development of low-profile and run-flat tyres, present different challenges even to experienced employees. Tyre repair and replacement should therefore only be tackled by competent staff. The main additional hazards which can arise during tyre repair and replacement are:

- manual handling injuries, which account for nearly a half of all tyre-related incidents reported (see Figure 22 for an example solution);
- tool-related injuries, particularly involving handtools such as tyre levers (accounting for a quarter of incidents); and
- compressed-air accidents related to an air blast from a ruptured or burst tyre or violent separation of the component parts of the wheel. Compressed-air accidents tend to result in serious injuries, including fatalities.

Figure 22 Using a tyre-lifting conveyor to reduce manual handling during storage

Car tyres

136 Before removing a road wheel, the area needs to be assessed to ensure that the vehicle will remain stable and safely supported and that traffic and people movements nearby do not pose a hazard. Check that the vehicle handbrake is on before the vehicle is jacked and chock all wheels that will remain in contact with the ground.

137 Experience from the car tyre-fitting industry has shown that where the floor is level, even and of known loading capacity, it may be acceptable to support the vehicle solely with a trolley jack suitable for lifting the weight of the vehicle in question.

138 In other circumstances it may be necessary to chock the wheels that will be in contact with the ground and use axle stands (chocks and stands will always be required if there is a need to gain access below or under the vehicle).

Figure 23 Use enough bead lubricant

Table 2 Removing and fitting car tyres

DO	DON'T
Loosen ('crack off') the wheel nuts on the wheel to be removed while it is still in contact with the ground	Don't remove wheel nuts completely until the wheel is raised
Remove the valve core to make sure the tyre is fully deflated before starting work on a tyre change or repair to a wheel	Don't store tyres horizontally – this can cause deformation that makes seating more difficult
Use enough bead lubricant when removing and fitting a tyre to a wheel rim (see Figure 23)	Don't use excessive force to remove a tyre or pressurise above its operating limit to force a fit
Examine wheels, tyres (externally and internally) and associated parts before fitting and particularly refitting after repair. Check to see if the wheel rim has a maximum pressure stamped on it	Don't refit tyres with visible damage or with non-specified parts
Use airline hoses long enough to allow the operator to stay outside the likely explosion trajectory during inflation (see Figure 24)	Don't use 'unrestricted' airlines (ie without a gauge or pressure control device) or valve connectors that require the operator to hold them in place
Use a calibrated torque wrench and follow the manufacturer's torque settings	Don't exceed the manufacturer's recommended tyre pressure for the size and rating of the tyre

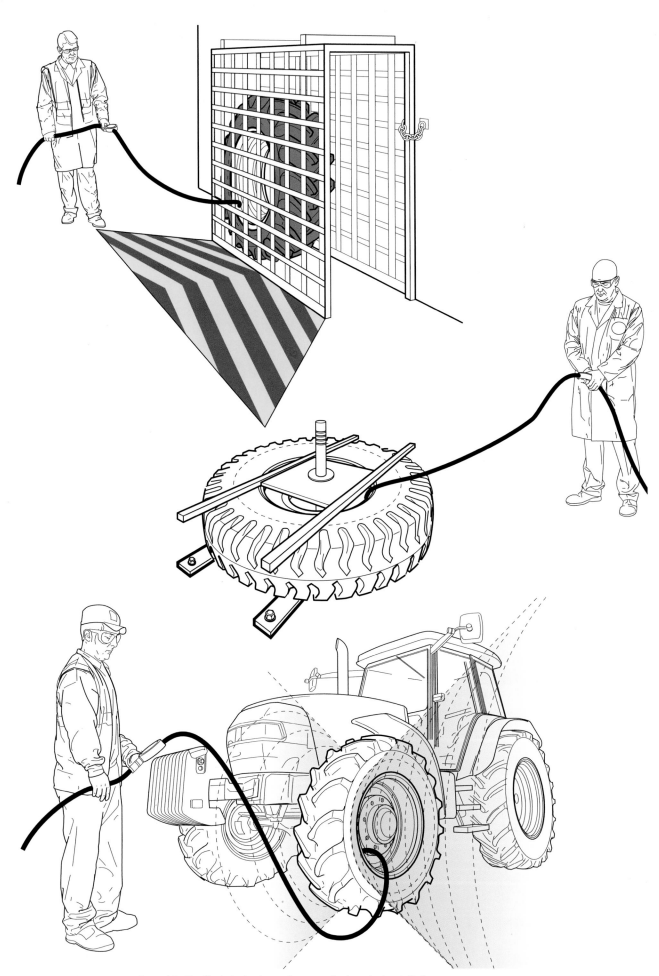

Figure 24 Always stand outside the likely trajectory of any explosion during inflation

Staying outside the likely explosion trajectory

139 Tyres contain a large amount of stored energy. For example, the sidewall of a typical commercial vehicle tyre has a surface area of around 2/3 m² (1000 square inches) and at 517 kPa (75 psi) the sidewall is withstanding over 34 tonnes of force. In the event of a failure, this force can be released explosively at an angle of up to 45 degrees from the rupture (which is often, but not always, the face of the sidewall).

140 There will be an increased risk of failure following tyre repair, when fitting a tyre to a split-rim wheel or where sidewall damage may be suspected (eg after a tyre has been run significantly underinflated). So the airline hose between the clip-on chuck and the pressure gauge/control should be long enough to allow the operator to stand outside the likely trajectory of any explosion during inflation. This will vary depending on the size of the tyre and its positioning.

Well-based wheels on commercial vehicles

141 This single-piece wheel is mainly used with tubeless tyres. Figures 25 and 26 show typical wheels used on heavy goods vehicles. Figure 27 is typical of a type used on light commercial vehicles. Tyre failure is occasionally experienced when inflating tyres of this type and can lead to a severe air blast. Safety measures include those for car tyres but include the additional precautions outlined in paragraphs 142 to 144.

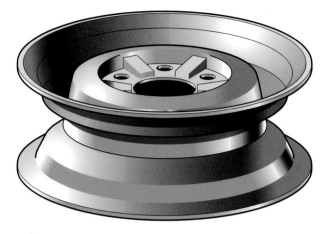

Figure 27 Well-based wheel used on light commercial vehicles

142 Use a restraining device when you are inflating above 15 psi, such as:

- a strong, firmly-secured cage (see Figure 29). Consider lining this with mesh to retain debris. For fixed installations it is helpful to mark the safety exclusion zone on the workshop floor as a reminder to staff (see Figure 24);
- a secured horizontal stool and associated clamping mechanism; or
- a portable restraint. These are available in the form of a lightweight cover (see Figure 28) that encloses the tyre and wheel rim and may be particularly advantageous for off-site repairs. With a bag restraint, in the event of an explosion the fabric expands and dissipates the blast while containing projected debris. Fabric devices may need to be replaced after an explosion.

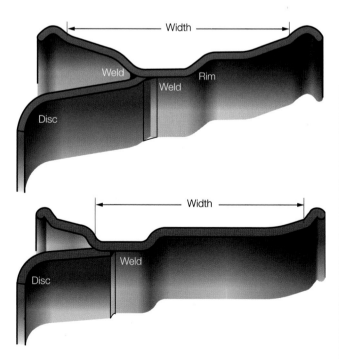

Figures 25 and 26 Typical well-based wheels used on heavy goods vehicles

Figure 28 A bag-type restraint

Figure 29 Wall-mounted inflation cage (photograph courtesy of ATS Euromaster Ltd)

143 During inflation the operator should not stand in the likely trajectory of the blast even when using a restraining device because they reduce but do not eliminate the risk. Airlines should be long enough (see paragraph 140) with quick-release couplings (see Figure 30) at both ends to allow the tyre to be deflated from outside the likely explosion trajectory if a fault (eg a potential 'zipper' failure of the sidewall) is suspected.

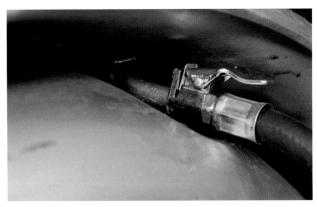

Figure 30 Clip-on chuck for tyre inflation

144 The pressure gauge/control valve should never be jammed in the open position, nor should 'unrestricted' airlines (ie without a gauge or pressure control device) be used to inflate any tyre. For bead-seating of large commercial tyres, removing the valve core allows faster inflation without using excessive pressure. Alternatively, using a 'bead blaster' device may be helpful when seating the tyre bead. Airlines attached to tyres should never be left unattended or connected long-term as air seepage may overinflate the tyre.

Split-rim wheels

145 Serious accidents, including fatalities, have been caused by the violent separation of split-rim wheels. They are becoming less common but may be encountered on older vehicles as well as military trucks, fork-lift trucks, cranes, scooters, caravans and wheelbarrows. They are also used for some off-road vehicles (because they allow the tyre to be removed without specialist equipment). Tyre removal/inflation should only be undertaken following the precautions set out below, which are in addition to those for car tyres.

146 There are two basic types of split-rim wheel assemblies:

- multi-piece wheels; and
- divided wheels.

Multi-piece wheels

147 This category includes large commercial wheels. The most common types are:

- the two-piece wheel (see Figure 31). A split-spring flange is fitted to a groove in the side of the wheel rim (known as the gutter groove) using levers. No locking ring is used;
- the three-piece wheel and four-piece wheel (see Figure 32). An endless flange and split locking ring are sprung into the gutter of the wheel rim using levers. Four-piece wheels use two endless flanges;
- demountable rims (see Figure 33). This is a three-piece, collapsible rim in which the disc is created by short spokes forming part of the hub.

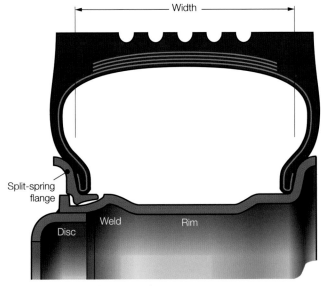

Figure 31 Two-piece wheel

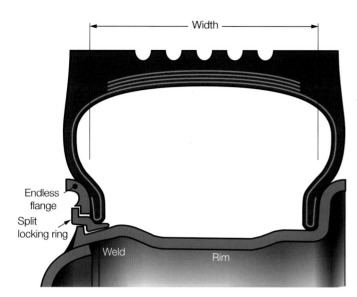

Width

Endless
flange

Split
locking ring

Weld

Rim

Figure 32 Three-piece wheel

Figure 33 Demountable rims

148 Failure of the locking ring/flange to seat correctly
can lead to violent separation of the component parts
of the wheel under pressure. Carefully check locking
rings and flanges before refitting and replace any that
are damaged. Lubricate the components according to
the manufacturer's instructions – do not hammer into
position. To ensure the loose components are properly
seated, inflate to no more than 15 psi with the fitter
outside the likely explosion trajectory. Final inflation
of such assembles should follow the precautions
in paragraphs 142 to 144, except that a bag-type
restraint is not designed for this type of assembly –
use a metal cage or frame instead.

Divided wheels

149 Divided wheels consist of two parts bolted
together with an outer ring of rim fasteners, the whole
assembly then being bolted to the vehicle hub by an
inner ring of hub studs (see Figures 34 and 35).

Figure 34 Divided wheel on a shovel loader showing two
bolts removed (the tyre was depressurised and the vehicle
was under maintenance)

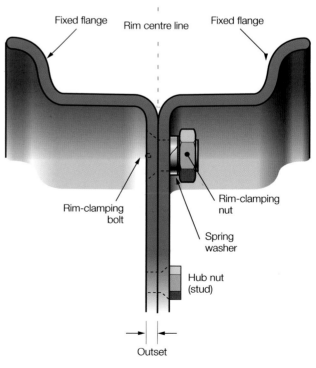

Fixed flange

Rim centre line

Fixed flange

Rim-clamping
bolt

Rim-clamping
nut

Spring
washer

Hub nut
(stud)

Outset

Figure 35 Cross-section of a divided wheel

150 Loosening the rim fasteners with the tyre under pressure has resulted in violent separation of rim halves, causing fatal injuries. Loosening the hub studs can have the same result if there has been damage or unauthorised repair to the wheel. Sometimes the rim-clamping nuts are painted in a contrasting colour to the rim to distinguish them.

151 Do not secure the rim-clamping bolts in position by welding the bolt head to one half of the wheel. This is likely to lead to weakening of the bolt, and if carried out with the tyre still on the wheel, may cause overheating resulting in explosion. Before taking a divided wheel off a vehicle you must ensure it is completely deflated and the valve core is removed.

152 If necessary, divided wheels should be inflated (with the fitter outside the likely explosion trajectory) to no more than 15 psi before fitting to the vehicle. All the rim and hub fasteners should then be correctly tightened so the wheel halves are fully clamped.

153 Follow the precautions in paragraphs 142 and 144 as applicable when inflating divided wheels on the vehicle. Where size permits, fit a suitable metal restraining device to contain the wheel components in the event of violent separation. If this is not possible, position the assembly in front of a protective barrier, eg a wall, embankment or the side of a vehicle. It is essential that people can work in a safe position.

Very large tyres

154 These are found on certain equipment used in construction, quarries, agriculture etc and pose additional hazards during repair. It may not be reasonably practicable to provide purpose-built cages of adequate strength, particularly for work on site. Restraint during tyre inflation is usually achieved by mounting on the wheel hub of the vehicle. Position the assembly in front of a protective barrier, such as a wall, embankment or the side of a vehicle, to restrain flying objects ejected during a failure. It is essential that people can work in a safe position.

155 Repair work on this type of tyre should only be carried out by staff who have had specific additional training. It is recommended that they are appointed in writing. As with all other wheels, hot work such as welding, or heating of seized components, should not be carried out with a tyre in position (inflated or deflated) as a severe explosion could result. This can be caused by ignition of hydrocarbon vapours within the tyre, resulting from the pyrolysis of the rubber of the tyre, or from the vaporisation of tyre lubricating grease or oil spilled onto the hub.

Manual handling of wheels and tyres

156 Manual handling injuries account for nearly a half of all tyre-related incidents reported. The average size of wheels and tyres has increased significantly, which creates a greater handling hazard because:

- the average weight has increased; and
- larger wheels and tyres are more difficult to hold and manoeuvre.

157 The Manual Handling Operations Regulations[13] require employers to avoid, where reasonably practicable, the need for employees to undertake manual handling tasks that involve a risk of injury. Given the variation in tasks undertaken in different MVR facilities, the risk of injury needs to be evaluated individually.

158 HSE has developed the manual handling assessment chart (MAC) tool to help users identify high-risk workplace manual handling activities. The tool can be used to assess the risks posed by lifting, carrying and team manual handling activities and is available free from HSE's website at www.hse.gov.uk/msd/mac.

159 Manual handling of tyres and wheels can be significantly reduced by using wheel lifts and tyre changers with integrated wheel lifters (see Figures 36 and 37). The repair of large tyres may require an appropriate mechanical handling system to allow manipulation so a full internal and external examination can be made to assess tyre damage. Extensive work has been done to develop tyre handling solutions. Further details can be found in paragraphs 308-316.

Figure 36 Wheel lifter

Tyre repair and replacement equipment

160 A variety of equipment is used in tyre repair, replacement and associated services such as wheel balancing. The hazards and precautions associated with the more common machinery are outlined below.

Bead breakers

161 Different types of bead breaker are used, which can be free-standing or combined with a tyre-changing machine. With the type shown in Figure 38, the tyre is clamped on a foot-operated revolving base. The seal may be broken by an air-operated spade or roller and an arm (which for modern run-flat tyres has hydraulic assistance), fitted with a tyre lever, removes each of the tyre beads from the wheel rim. Fitting the tyre is the reverse operation, using a different tool on the end of the lever.

162 The machine has the potential to trap operator's fingers and precautions should be taken to prevent them from being distracted, for example by positioning the machine away from main thoroughfares. It is important that the operator is competent and keeps up to date with changes in tyre and wheel rim design.

Figure 38 Tyre changer showing the use of a bead clamp

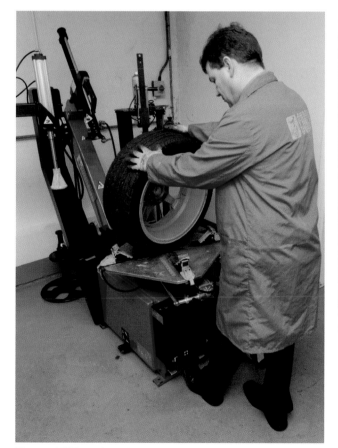

Figure 37 Tyre-changing machine with integrated wheel lift

Figure 39 An asymmetrical wheel showing subtly differing well profile

For example, Figure 39 shows an asymmetrical wheel with a subtly different well profile on the left-hand side compared to the right, which determines how the tyre is removed and replaced.

163 On those machines where the foot used to refit tyres incorporates a roller, regular checks should be carried out to ensure that it rotates freely and has not been affected by tyre/soap deposits etc. Failing to do so may lead to tyre or wheel damage or failure of the roller.

Wheel-balancing machines

164 There are various designs of wheel-balancing machine, which may be manually or mechanically rotated (see Figure 40 for one example). An out-of-balance spinning wheel and tyre creates a fluctuating force that is detected by sensors. The machine is stopped and the appropriate weights are applied to the rim.

165 The hazards associated with mechanically powered machines are largely due to the speed of rotation and motor torque. Before each wheel is balanced, it should be checked for loose stones,

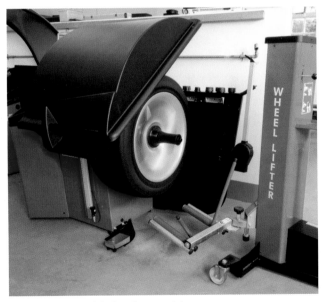

Figure 40 Wheel-balancing machine

weights etc that could fly off. Wheel-balancer driveshafts and the rotating road wheel should be effectively guarded to reduce the possibility of clothing getting caught.

166 Where there is sufficient torque or rotational energy to cause injury, machines should be fitted with an interlocked cover that protects the wheel while it is in motion and will brake the wheel if it is lifted. Check the guard at regular intervals to make sure it is operating correctly. The electrical controls should be positioned so that the operator does not have to reach across the machine to use them. Storage of any wheel-balancing tools or replacement parts should not interfere with the safe operation of the machine.

Puncture repair

167 British Standard BS AU159f *Specification for repairs to tyres for motor vehicles used on the public highway*[14] provides useful information for assessing the suitability of a damaged tyre for repair and procedures for carrying out repairs. Minor puncture repairs can be carried out using cold cure systems. This involves 'vulcanising' – a precured rubber plug is inserted into

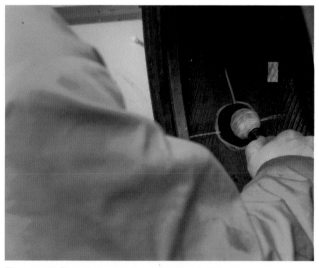

Figure 41 Puncture repair – abrading inside tyre

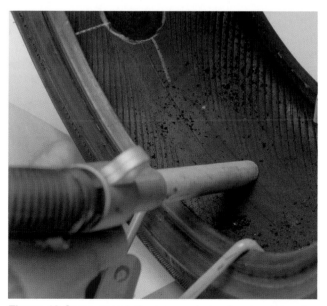

Figure 42 Compressed-air vacuum device for cleaning out rubber dust. (See also Figure 68)

the hole in the tyre casing, using rubber solution. Before patching, the inside surface of the casing is buffed, typically using a pneumatic handtool fitted with a wire brush or an abrasive wheel (see Figure 41). A buff cleaning solution (generally a mixed hydrocarbon solvent) is then applied. The main hazards associated with this work are as follows.

Exposure to solvent fume from cleaning and rubber solutions

- Where small quantities are applied by brush, you can generally achieve adequate control by good standards of general ventilation in the working area. If solvent is sprayed, local exhaust ventilation may be required.
- Skin contact with solvents and adhesives should be avoided; nitrile gloves should be sufficient to provide short-term protection.

Exposure to dust from buffing operations

- Where there is heavy use of buffing equipment, local exhaust ventilation is preferable – this may be integral to the hand-buffing tool, but more usually a flexible section of ducting is inserted into the casing close to the area being buffed.
- Only where this is not reasonably practicable should you rely on using suitable RPE.
- Abraded dust should not be blown from inside the tyre casing with a compressed airline as this makes the dust airborne – a vacuum device or similarly effective work procedure should be used instead (see Figure 42).
- Flying rubber particles present a risk of eye injury and suitable eye protection should be worn during buffing operations.

168 Assess the extent of exposure to solvent fume and rubber dust, together with the adequacy of the control measures on an individual basis, as required by COSHH. Where puncture repair work is intermittent and of short duration, as at most MVR facilities, good standards of general ventilation should be adequate.

169 An alternative method of puncture repair uses an uncured rubber patch or plug that is cured using electrically heated pressure pads. Ensure there is adequate ventilation to remove any significant rubber fume generated.

170 Increasingly, vehicle manufacturers are supplying post-puncture tyre sealants as a replacement for spare tyres, and pre-puncture sealants are used in horticultural applications. Make sure that adequate control measures are in place to protect against contact with the sealants and inhalation of solvents or propellants.

Roadside repairs and recovery

Road traffic incidents (RTIs) and work-related safety

171 People at work on the roadside, either recovering or repairing motor vehicles (which includes tyre and windscreen replacement), are subject to an additional risk – from other road users. Many RTIs are not reportable to HSE, but it is estimated that there could be up to ten RTI deaths to people engaged in roadside recovery/repair each year.

172 Working at the roadside creates additional hazards, which may be site-specific and require dynamic ('on-the-spot') risk assessments to be carried out. In some circumstances, it may be safer to tow the vehicle to a workshop than attempt a roadside repair.

173 Protecting workers and members of the public from traffic risks on public roads is mostly a matter for road traffic law, which is enforced by the police and other agencies. However, existing health and safety legislation requires employers and self-employed people to protect workers and safeguard others put at risk by their work activities. For example, they should:

- provide safe systems of work to ensure the safety of workers and the occupants of vehicles being recovered/repaired;
- ensure vehicles and/or attachments, eg winches, cranes etc, are subject to examination or inspection under health and safety legislation, even though they are not covered by MOT testing.

Essential precautions

174 It is important to ensure that:

- you assess all risks properly (traffic conditions, weather, lighting, road surface and camber if jacking the vehicle etc) and prepare safe systems for working at the roadside – including where and how you park your vehicle (see Figure 44). The fend-off position is generally considered the best vehicle orientation and should be used unless factors in the dynamic risk assessment indicate it is inappropriate;

- you provide and maintain vehicles and equipment of an appropriate standard;
- appropriate personal protective equipment (PPE), eg high-visibility (see BS EN 471:2003 *High-visibility warning clothing for professional use*)[15] and weatherproof clothing, footwear and gloves, is provided and used. Mobile workers will also require a first-aid kit and a means of communication (eg a mobile phone);
- employees have been adequately trained by a competent trainer to work safely at the roadside and to advise people in casualty vehicles on the precautions they should be taking. Specialist training courses are commercially available;
- employees don't try to handle any hazardous substances, or do specialist work, unless they have received appropriate training and have access to the necessary equipment (including protective clothing). For example, vehicles with significant structural damage may create additional risks, from escape of fuel or exposure to high-voltage or stored electrical energy in electric hybrid vehicles (see paragraphs 349-354).

Repair or recovery of buses and coaches fitted with air suspension

175 For many years, passenger service vehicles (PSVs) have been fitted with rubber bellows (also known as airbags) supplied with air from the vehicle's air compressor. These allow the height to be varied to suit certain needs, for example lowering the step for improved access.

176 A characteristic of air suspension is that vehicle ground clearance can suddenly and unexpectedly change due to a drop in air pressure. This presents crushing and trapping hazards to technicians recovering or repairing vehicles, especially if working beneath them (see Figure 43).

Figure 43 Limited clearance beneath vehicle even with bellows inflated

177 The risk of this happening is significantly reduced if two basic principles are adopted:

- Never crawl beneath a vehicle fitted with air suspension unless it is properly supported.
- Never tamper with the ride height for the purposes of recovery or repair.

178 It should be possible to follow these principles if the task is adequately planned and enough time is allowed (ie recovery operatives should not be pressurised to take short cuts). Sufficient planning means that:

- the risks associated with each task are adequately assessed;
- each task is explained so the technician understands it fully. Their roles and responsibilities must be clearly understood, as well as those of their colleagues;
- all technicians have specific knowledge of the affected vehicle and carry the necessary equipment to undertake the job safely;
- the technician arrives with a suitable recovery vehicle (if recovery is necessary);
- working procedures are planned and well rehearsed;
- equipment is in a safe condition by virtue of adequate inspection, maintenance and examination and has been subject to statutory examination;
- technicians know which procedures to follow if their training and instructions do not cover the situation encountered;
- documentation should be in place to ensure that all of the above measures, controls and plans are correctly implemented.

Guidance on training and equipment

179 The British Standards Institution (BSI) has published a number of priced documents containing guidelines on both the standard of training and equipment specifications, for example:

- PAS 43:2008 *Safe working of vehicle breakdown, recovery and removal operations: Management system specification;*[16]
- BS 7121-12:1999 *Safe use of cranes. Part 12: Recovery vehicles and equipment. Code of Practice.*[17] Contains guidelines and recommendations for ensuring the health and safety of people at work and members of the public during recovery operations;
- BS 7901:2002 *Specification for recovery vehicles and vehicle recovery equipment.*[18] Specifies performance requirements for recovery equipment for moving casualty vehicles during breakdown or recovery activities.

Further information is given in HSE guidance:

- *Safe recovery (and repair) of buses and coaches fitted with air suspension;*[19]
- *Driving at work: Managing work-related road safety;*[20]
- *Safe working with vehicle air-conditioning systems;*[7]
- *Safe working with LPG-fuelled motor vehicles.*[21]

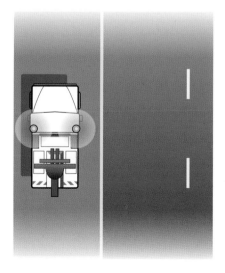
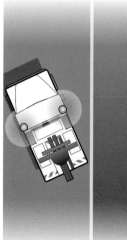

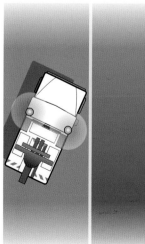

In line   Fend in   Fend off

Figure 44 Positioning of recovery/repair vehicle: in line; fend in; and fend off

Automotive glazing

180 Repair and replacement of glazing is extremely common and often carried out away from the company premises. As with all unsupervised mobile operations, instruction and training are key factors to safe working.

181 Particular hazards include:

■ cuts from broken glass or cutting tools (see Figure 45);
■ manual handling injuries (commercial vehicle and public service vehicle glazing can weigh up to 100 kg, and access to the windscreen area of the vehicle can be difficult);
■ working at height;
■ contact with hazardous chemicals (eg sealants);
■ environmental hazards (working at the roadside, adverse weather etc).

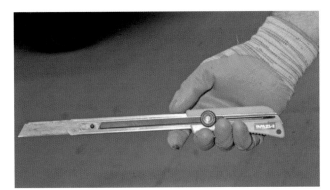

Figure 45 'Long knives' are responsible for numerous serious accidents – use a safer alternative

182 The employer (or self-employed technician) needs to assess the foreseeable risks of particular operations. However, while some risks may be anticipated, others may arise in individual circumstances and require a risk assessment to be carried out at the time of each job. Mobile technicians will need to be trained in on-site risk assessment.

183 The ability to install a particular screen without undue risk of a manual handling injury to the technician will depend on:

■ the weight and shape of the glass;
■ the height from the floor and angle of the vehicle aperture, which determines the arm extension and posture required by the technician to position the glass;
■ the individual capabilities of the person;
■ other factors such as wind loading.

184 In some circumstances a single-person lift will be unacceptable and a lifting device or a second person will be required.

Figure 46 Lifting device used to accurately position a replacement screen

185 Where work at height is required, a suitable access platform should be used. The platform should have sufficient stability and be capable of supporting the load of two people and the screen.

186 Technicians will normally require the following PPE:

■ safety footwear;
■ cut-resistant, eg Kevlar, gloves (see Figure 47) and sleeves;
■ suitable eye protection;
■ chemically resistant gloves (eg disposable nitrile);
■ mobile technicians will also require a high-visibility vest (see BS EN 471:2003 *High-visibility warning clothing for professional use*);[15]
■ weatherproof clothing;
■ a first-aid kit and a means of communication (eg mobile phone).

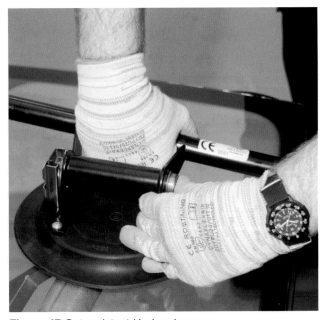

Figure 47 Cut-resistant Kevlar gloves

Common issues in MVR

Starting, moving and road testing vehicles

187 Engines should only be started by someone sitting in the driver's seat with their legs in the vehicle, with the handbrake on and the vehicle in neutral gear. Failing to follow this procedure, for example operating the starter motor from outside the vehicle, has resulted in fatal injuries due to the vehicle falling from a lift, running over a worker beneath it or crushing someone as an open door passes a support pillar, adjacent vehicle or other fixed object.

188 Vehicle movements are an obvious hazard in MVR. They may involve customers driving onto an unfamiliar site or workers transferring vehicles in and out of a busy workshop with restricted access or visibility. To reduce the risk:

- make somebody responsible for vehicle movement and testing and allow only fully trained, licensed, responsible drivers to move/test vehicles, particularly high-performance cars;
- ensure visiting drivers and customers are aware of your rules;
- keep keys secure when vehicles are not in use;
- supervise vehicle movements in restricted spaces, near blind corners and especially when reversing (see paragraphs 414-418);
- ensure people authorised to drive automatic vehicles are familiar with their operation, especially if they have been adapted.

Under-vehicle access

189 Whenever anyone enters the space beneath a vehicle they are at risk, although the type of risk depends on whether the vehicle is elevated or on the level.

Vehicle elevated

190 There have been serious and fatal accidents when a lifted vehicle has fallen onto a worker, eg due to failure of the lifting equipment, or due to the vehicle falling from it. Common factors are incorrect installation or inadequate inspection and maintenance.

191 Choose lifting equipment carefully to make sure it is suitable for the vehicle. Vehicle-lifting devices should only be used by authorised and trained staff, as special care is needed when manoeuvring vehicles, positioning chocks, jacks and props, and to prevent overloading. Even simple, common items like jacks and axle stands need to be adequately maintained. Regular inspection and maintenance of all lifting equipment is required and records should be kept available.

192 Vehicle lifts should have effective hold-to-run controls that are clearly marked to indicate their function and be fitted with automatic anti-fallback protection. Toe traps should also be avoided – including when body-straightening jigs are fitted. A raised platform should not be used as a working area unless proper working balconies or platforms with barrier rails are provided and the platform surface provides reasonable grip.

Vehicle lifts

193 There are many types of vehicle lift incorporating different means of hoisting. The most common have two or four posts, but other designs, for example single-, three- or six-post; scissor etc, can be found in service (see Figure 48). Lifts are often provided with special attachments which allow axles, wheels etc to be removed.

195 All-round protection for both surface and recessed lifts should be provided to prevent toe-trapping injuries between the lift platform and the floor (see Figure 50). If the lift is fitted into a recess, it can be 'blocked-up' (ie physically prevented from fully lowering to the ground) to provide clearance for toes beneath the moving structure.

Figure 48 Six-synchronised mobile lifts

194 Where possible, vehicle lifts should comply with the relevant British/European Standards (see paragraph 196). Vehicle lifts that were manufactured before CE Marking should be adapted to meet the following requirements – each lift should:

- show the maximum working load in a conspicuous place, with letters not less than 50 mm high;
- be positioned so that any moving part is a minimum of 600 mm from the nearest fixed structure;
- have all-round toe protection;
- operate by hold-to-run controls;
- have a suitable method of electrical isolation;
- have chocks or end-stops to prevent a vehicle rolling off the lift (see Figure 49);
- be fitted with arm-locking devices where appropriate.

Figure 49 Hinged end-stops help prevent the vehicle falling from the lift when elevated

Figure 50 Four-post lift with recessed floor

196 If this is not possible, toe protection may be provided by using the clearance measurements in BS 7980:2003 *Vehicle lifts. Installation, maintenance, thorough examination and safe use. Code of practice*[22] and BS EN 1493:1999 *Vehicle lifts*[23] (see Figure 51).

Figure 52 Toe clearance on a vehicle lift

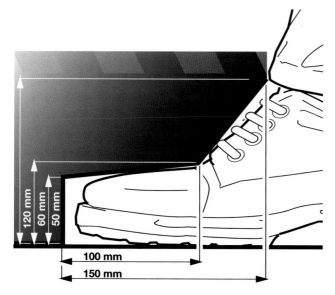

Figure 51 Dimensions for toe clearance on a vehicle lift

197 Toe protection can also be achieved if, during the lowering of the lift, the movement is automatically halted (eg at a distance of 120 mm) before the danger position (see Figure 52). The movement can then be restarted by operating an additional lowering control or by releasing and reactivating the normal lowering control. The final portion of the travel should be accompanied by an audible warning. In either case it should not be possible to override the stopping device so that the lift travels to its initial position without stopping.

Two-post lifts

198 Two-post lifts typically consist of two upright columns: a master or powered column, plus an auxiliary or 'slave', both fitted with a pair of (vehicle) carrying arms. These arms are pivoted at the column and their lengths are adjustable, usually by telescopic means, though some are articulated. At the free end of each carrying arm there is an adjustable pick-up plate fitted with a rubber mounting pad. A two-post lift achieves 'wheel-free lifting' by aligning the pick-up plates to four jacking points on the underside of the chassis of the vehicles. It is important that:

- you follow the vehicle manufacturer's recommendations regarding vehicle lifting. In particular, you need to ensure the equipment is suitable when lifting larger SUV and 'light' freight and commercial vans (LCVs);

- vehicle chassis and chassis jack points are identifiable and in a satisfactory condition. Vehicle jacking points are usually identified by a symbol on the vehicle sill, if in doubt always consult the car handbook;
- the support-arm rubber mounting pads are in serviceable condition and, where necessary, for example to avoid the lift arm fouling the car bodywork, are set at the correct height before the vehicle is raised;
- the lifting arms are carefully positioned before each lift (see Figure 53), in accordance with the manufacturer's instructions. This is to ensure correct weight distribution and proper contact with load-bearing points so the vehicle is stable. Also take account of the weight distribution of the vehicle, eg front/rear engined, loads within vehicle/boot, and absence of major components such as engine or gearbox;
- you consider the effect on the stability of the vehicle caused by the removal of major components or by the application of forces, via tools etc;
- the lift arms are fitted with an effective automatic mechanical arm locking system to maintain the angle between them. These should be checked regularly – typically daily.

Figure 53 Always ensure correct adjustment of two-post lift arms for the vehicle being lifted

199 It is essential that two-post lifts are installed correctly into a suitable base. This is particularly important where the posts are free-standing (with no bridging support). Specialist advice may be required to ensure the structural integrity of the floor and fixings and the lift supplier or specialist garage equipment maintenance company should be consulted.

Single-post mini-lifts

200 Single-post mini-lifts, as in Figure 54, should be treated in the same way as vehicle jacks, ie access should not be allowed beneath the lifted vehicle unless supplemented by suitable supports such as props (see paragraphs 207-210).

Figure 54 Single-post mini-lift

Jacks (including trolley jacks)

201 There is a history of fatal and serious injuries caused by the failure of jacks. While many possess built-in safeguards, their simplicity and mobility may make their operators complacent. Take the following precautions when using jacks to lift or support vehicles:

- never work beneath a vehicle supported only by a jack or jacks;
- the correct jack for the job should be used. It should be capable of taking the load of the vehicle to be lifted and be applied to the correct jacking point of its underside, as identified by the vehicle manufacturer;

- the jack should not be relied upon as the sole support if work is to take place beneath the vehicle or if more than one axle is raised. It should be supplemented with appropriate stands, and the wheels of the vehicle still in contact with the ground should be chocked (see Figure 55);
- jacks should only be used on firm, level ground;
- scheduled routine inspection and maintenance should be carried out to ensure jacks are in good working order; and
- operators should be trained in their correct use.

Figure 55 Car with trolley jack and axle stand

Thorough examination of vehicle-lifting devices

202 Vehicle-lifting devices are subject to the requirements of the Lifting Operations and Lifting Equipment Regulations 1998 (LOLER).[24] They will generally be exposed to conditions causing deterioration, which can result in dangerous situations and will require examination at the frequencies suggested below (or in accordance with a written examination scheme prepared by a competent person). Records of examination should be kept for at least two years.

203 Because people will almost invariably either work beneath or be inside a vehicle raised on a lift, the lifts should be subject to thorough examination every six months.

204 Many body alignment jigs used in body repairs have features similar to those of vehicle lifts. Similar considerations will apply, but where people do not regularly work underneath jigs a 12-monthly period for thorough examination may be appropriate.

205 Garage equipment such as trolley and bottle jacks should be regarded as lifting equipment, with thorough examination every 12 months.

Vehicle supports

Ramps
206 These are usually fixed in position. A short, portable version will merely maintain a vehicle in a tilted position, while a longer ramp will enable a vehicle to attain an elevated horizontal position (see Figure 56). The ramps have no moving parts and safety in their use is achieved through their intrinsic design/strength, along with commonsense procedures such as careful manoeuvring of vehicles, and braking/chocking of wheels.

Figure 56 Purpose-built lorry ramp

Props
207 These are essential items of equipment. When used properly, they make it safer for people to work beneath vehicles that have been raised by lifting devices such as trolley jacks.

208 Props may be used to support a raised vehicle in a wheel-free condition, after the vehicle has been lifted by a number of jacks. They should only be used on firm, level ground and should be designed to adequately carry the loads placed on them.

209 A common type of prop is the axle stand or axle tree. When supplied, such equipment is provided with the appropriate pins to adjust the height of the stand. When these pins are lost or damaged replace them with close-fitting pins of the correct specification, and not screwdrivers, bolts, or other items of unknown load capacity. Inspect the structure and integrity of the axle stand, especially welded joint areas, regularly.

210 The cabs of some heavy goods vehicles can be tilted forward to allow access to the engine and other vehicle parts. They are commonly fitted with a prop, which should be locked in position before gaining access, as in Figure 57. Similarly, the load area of some goods vehicles can be elevated (eg tipper lorries) and if access is needed below them they should be effectively propped (see Figure 58).

Figure 58 Props for a tipper lorry

Examination of vehicle supports

211 The safe operation of a vehicle support is dependent on its condition in use, and deterioration would lead to a significant risk to the operator or other worker. They should be inspected, as required by the Provision and Use of Work Equipment Regulations 1998 (PUWER),[25] typically every 12 months. Keep a record of the results until the next inspection.

Vehicle on the level

212 Access can be gained under a vehicle that remains on the level on its road wheels, either from a pit or by crawling or sliding underneath it. For a vehicle that remains on its road wheels, there is a risk that it could be driven away. Before work commences, where possible, the starting control should be removed from the vehicle and retained by the worker gaining under-vehicle access (eg take the keys out of the ignition). If access is necessary with the starting control active, eg to operate the engine or the power steering, it is important to operate a safe system of work, particularly if two or more people are working on the vehicle.

213 Where access is gained under a vehicle which remains on its road wheels and is fitted with pneumatic suspension (eg some buses) there is a risk of a serious or fatal accident if the suspension is deflated, either due to catastrophic failure or inadvertent deflation. People carrying out such work should be trained and competent. Further guidance is given in paragraphs 175-178.

Figure 57 Prop for an HGV cab

Inspection pits

214 Inspection pits are still commonly found in MVR premises and an assessment of workplace risks may well show that they are the safest option when working on diesel-fuelled vehicles. But they present particular hazards and are a common cause of accidents, not only to those unfamiliar with the premises but also to employees who momentarily forget the presence of an unfenced pit, or who slip or trip, and fall into them. When working on petrol-fuelled vehicles, a lift is usually a safer alternative.

215 The principal hazards are:

- falling into the pit (the Work at Height Regulations will apply, see paragraphs 368-378);
- slipping on access steps;
- fire or asphyxiation from an accumulation of gases or vapours that are heavier than air, or fuel release;
- a vehicle or other objects falling on an employee in the pit;
- head injuries from contact with the vehicle over the pit.

Preventing falls into pits

216 When deciding on the precautions, the employer needs to consider a number of options. The best solution is likely to depend on the particular work undertaken, layout of the premises and management and supervision in the workplace. It will probably include a combination of measures drawn from the hierarchy in paragraphs 217-224.

Limiting access to the area

217 The more people working or walking around the pit area, the greater the risk of falls, probably because they become familiar with the risk and are concentrating on other tasks. Restrict access to people who need to be there. Where possible, physically segregate the pit or group of pits or modify the layout of the workplace to keep non-authorised people away from the pit area (for example by making clearly defined pedestrian routes and using barriers and partitions, as in Figure 59). Provide enough signs and supervision to enforce this segregation.

Covering pit openings

218 Where practical, cover pit openings when they are not in use. Also cover areas of the pit that are left exposed when the vehicle being worked on is shorter than the length of the pit. A number of proprietary systems are available that allow all or parts of the pit to be covered, as in Figures 60, 61 and 62.

219 Ideally, any cover should:

- be quick to install and remove (for example if a pit worker needs to get out in an emergency);
- be robust enough to withstand a falling person and any other load likely to be imposed on them;
- fit securely in place;
- be compatible with other pit equipment.

Figure 59 Chained-off entrance and warning signs outside pit area

Figure 60 Metal lattice pit covers (photograph courtesy of Oxford Safety Components Ltd)

220 Installation and removal of covers may itself create a small risk, due to handling and proximity to the opening, and this should be weighed against the time that the pit is left uncovered and other precautions in place.

Figure 61 Reinforced fabric cover being fixed in place (photograph courtesy of Everquip Garage Equipment Ltd)

Figure 62 Motorised pit cover (photograph courtesy of Premier Pits Ltd)

Safe access across the pit

221 Given the length of many pits, people take short cuts across the opening even where there are 'official' instructions not to. It may be a better solution to provide a proprietary moveable bridge across the pit with handrails on the open sides (see Figure 63). Such a bridge can also be used as a safe platform for work that would otherwise be impractical to carry out due to the open pit, for example on the rear engine of a bus or coach.

Figure 63 Moveable bridge allowing access across middle of pit

Other types of barrier

222 Guard rails, chains or extendible barriers can provide flexible protection for workers near the pit edge (see Figure 64). They allow access to the side of a vehicle over a pit (as the vehicle covers the pit at this point) while providing a warning of the open pit not covered by the vehicle. They need to be sufficiently high, stable and clearly visible so that they do not create a tripping hazard. Extendible barriers are not designed to withstand the weight of a falling person, but act as a physical reminder of an open edge.

Improving visibility

223 It is important that the pit opening can be seen easily. Use pit lighting during working hours and clearly mark pit edges, for example by black and yellow bands of slip-resistant paint. Ensure the pit lights are kept clean and replace failed bulbs immediately. White painted walls help reflect light and increase the efficiency of the lighting system, but need to be cleaned regularly.

Figure 64 Pit bridge with one handrail removed to provide access to the rear of a bus. Extendible barriers provide a warning about the open area of the pit

Reducing the risk of slips and trips

224 Ensure the surface around the pit is slip-resistant, either by using anti-slip materials or by having an effective cleaning regime. As far as possible, keep the area clear from obstructions and deal with spillages immediately. Similarly, keep the area inside the pit free from obstructions – this will improve access for pit workers.

Access to pits

225 Pits require safe means of entry and exit. Provide at least one fixed entry/exit point with additional, separate, usable means of escape where the risk assessment identifies the need (for example, where escape may be blocked off by the parked vehicle or for pits over 9 m long).

226 A significant number of injuries occur from people slipping on the access steps. Provide a handrail where possible, for example a permanent handrail may be

appropriate on sunken pits or low-level handrails below floor level. Removable handrails may be an option for other installations, as in Figure 65.

Figure 65 Handrail can be temporarily removed on drive-through pits (photograph courtesy of Everquip Garage Equipment Ltd)

227 Use slip-resistant coatings on the steps and keep them free from contamination. The Health and Safety Laboratory (HSL) have carried out extensive research on tread patterns for footwear, which shows large variations in performance even for those designated 'slip-resistant'. When specifying footwear, remember that 'oil-resistant' does not mean 'slip-resistant'. See paragraphs 421-424 for further details.

Preventing fire and asphyxiation

228 Pits are likely to have poor natural ventilation so the release of any low flashpoint substance or heavier-than-air gas above or near a pit can create fire/explosion and asphyxiation risks. To reduce these risks:

■ do not carry out pit work on non-diesel tanks or associated fuel lines where there is a risk of release. Do not carry out any hot work on or near any tank or fuel line, including diesel systems;

■ do not store portable LPG heaters, or other LPG-fuelled devices, in or near pits in case they leak;

■ before carrying out pit work on air-conditioning units, empty the refrigerant with a proprietary system well away from the pit area;

■ do not weld in a pit unless effective local exhaust ventilation is provided;

■ use fixed lighting in the pit that is suitable for potentially explosive atmospheres and conforms to a suitable standard;

■ use handlamps of special construction, that have been designed and tested to prevent ignition in flammable atmospheres (see paragraphs 266-283 for further details);

■ do not leave vehicles idling over pits unless there is dedicated exhaust extraction.

Preventing vehicles or other objects falling into the pit

229 Highlighted pit edges (approximately 150 mm wide) are a useful guide when driving vehicles on and off the pit but may need supplementing with mirrors. It may be necessary to authorise a competent marshal to assist manoeuvring (and watch out for moving vehicles or pedestrians). Only competent and authorised drivers should be allowed to manoeuvre vehicles on and off the pit.

230 For narrow-wheelbase, twin-wheeled vehicles (where the inner tyre may be hanging over the pit edge), ensure that the outer tyres are correctly inflated and in a satisfactory condition to reduce the risk of vehicles tipping or sliding into the pit. Also ensure that outer tyres will not be loaded in excess of their carrying capacity (load index rating).

231 Remove discarded or replaced parts as soon as possible and do not leave tools or other items around the pit apron, working platforms etc.

Preventing other injuries

232 Provide suitable head protection for pit workers where there is a risk of injury from contact with the vehicle overhead or from falling objects. The ultimate strength of the head protection is probably less important than the ability to wear it. For example, baseball-style, short-peak bump caps provide a degree of protection, stay in place and allow reasonable upward vision (see Figure 66). They may be more appropriate than traditional, construction-type helmets. Eye protection may be required to guard against displaced dust, rust or other debris and especially materials ejected under pressure, eg hydraulic fluids. Ear defenders may be necessary for noisy processes such as engine running.

Figure 66 Adequate lighting and clean, reflective walls provide good illumination. Protective equipment includes bump cap, coveralls, gloves and safety footwear

Compressed-air equipment

233 Compressed air is used for a variety of purposes including:

- inflating tyres;
- for spray guns and air-fed breathing apparatus;
- supplying pneumatic handtools, grease guns etc;
- supplying air to pneumatic tyre removers.

234 Accidents, some of which have been fatal, occur when the energy contained in a pressurised container is released with explosive force or where compressed air is injected into the body.

235 All compressed-air plant and systems must be designed, constructed and installed to prevent danger. Ensure there is a maintenance programme for the whole pressure system. It should take into account the system and equipment age, its uses and the environment.

236 The pressure system should be subject to a written scheme of examination agreed by a competent person, which covers:

- every pressure vessel;
- all protective devices; and
- those parts of pipelines and pipework which, if they fail, may create danger.

237 A competent person must examine the pressure system in accordance with the written scheme and records must be kept.

238 Where pressure testing is necessary, use hydraulic pressure with suitable precautions rather than compressed air and, if possible, when leak testing components not intended as pressure vessels, eg vehicle fuel tanks and radiators.

239 The pressure of the compressed air supplied from the receiver should be as low as practicable. Where there is a big difference in the pressures required (eg between air guns and bead breakers), separate lines should be used through reducing valves and an associated safety valve (see Figure 67). Where possible, use different designs of connectors to ensure that a low-pressure item cannot be connected to the high-pressure line. Where this is not possible, the supply points should be clearly labelled and colour coded. Water traps should be provided in all lines.

Figure 67 Compressed-air supply showing water separator, regulator and two-stage release safety couplings

240 Flexible airlines can be subject to physical damage and may deteriorate over time. This can cause them to rupture, particularly at connection points, which can lead to sudden discharge of compressed air and may cause unsupported lengths of hose to 'whip' or 'snake' dangerously. All airlines should be checked frequently for signs of damage or deterioration.

241 Hoses above 10 mm bore, more than 10 m long, or subject to a pressure over 7 bar, should be fitted with a coupling which has a self-venting socket. The socket should release any downstream pressure before allowing disconnection. Another way of reducing 'whipping' or 'snaking' is to fit emergency shut-off valves, hose rupture valves or air fuses as close as practicable to the connector. The valves will close or reduce flow to a very low level in the event of excessive airflow conditions caused by a failure of the hose.

242 The pressure gauges and compressed-air metering devices should be inspected regularly, ie once a month. The drive and other moving parts of the compressor should be guarded to prevent all hand and finger access to the dangerous parts from any direction.

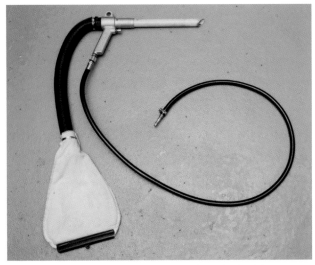

Figure 68 Vacuum device (uses the Venturi principle to convert compressed air to suction)

243 Compressed air should never be used to blow away filings, chips, dust etc. Devices are available that can be fitted to compressed airlines, which suck rather than blow and contain the contaminant (see Figure 68).

244 Accidental or deliberate injection of material and/or compressed air, either through the skin or into a body orifice, may cause injuries that can be fatal. Internal organs rupture at low pressures in comparison with those of compressed airlines. Ordinary working clothes do not significantly restrict the penetration of compressed air into the body and no one should use compressed air to dust themselves down. Employees should be made aware of the hazards and warned of the potential consequences of horseplay.

245 Take care to avoid accidental injections when using compressed-air equipment, particularly in awkward or confined situations such as inside or beneath vehicles, and when clearing or cleaning paint spray guns. Always seek medical advice after compressed-air penetration occurs or is suspected because the degree of injury is not always immediately apparent. Further advice is given in HSE's guidance booklet *Compressed air safety*.[26]

Noise and vibration

Noise exposure

246 Prolonged and excessive exposure to noise is a serious health hazard. It accelerates the normal hearing loss we get as we grow older and can cause a permanent sensation of ringing in the ears, known as tinnitus. Less-obvious side effects – increased pulse rate, blood pressure and breathing rate – indicate that noise (and vibration) causes stress.

247 Noise is measured in decibels (dB). An increase of 3 dB doubles the noise, so what might seem a small difference in noise level may be a large difference in exposure. If the noise is so loud that you have to raise your voice to speak to someone 2 metres away, it may be loud enough to damage your hearing.

248 When assessing whether there is a problem with noise in the workplace, remember that:

■ hearing loss caused by noise exposure at work is preventable but once your hearing has been damaged, it won't come back;
■ both the level of noise and how long people are exposed to it contribute to hearing damage;
■ modifying work practice can be an efficient and effective way of controlling noise at source, eg changes in process, reducing vibration (damping), replacing ageing machinery and reducing time spent in noisy areas;
■ health surveillance is vital to detect and respond to early signs of hearing loss.

249 The Control of Noise at Work Regulations[27] put duties on employers and the self-employed to assess and identify measures to eliminate or reduce risks from exposure (see Table 3).

Table 3 Managing noise exposure

Level of exposure	Management actions
Lower-exposure action values: Daily (or weekly) exposure of 80 dB(A) Peak sound pressure of 135 dB(C)	Appoint a competent person to assess the risk to workers' health Provide employees with information and training Provide hearing protection if requested, ie earmuffs or earplugs Provide health surveillance for groups at special risk
Upper-exposure action values: Daily (or weekly) exposure of 85 dB(A) Peak sound pressure of 137 dB(C)	Reduce exposure to as low a level as reasonably practicable through organisational and technical measures Provide hearing protection and ensure it is used (employees have a duty to wear the protection provided) Demarcate hearing protection zones – ensure no one enters unless wearing hearing protection Provide health surveillance
Exposure limit values: Daily or weekly exposure of 87 dB(A) Peak sound pressure of 140 dB(C)	These exposure limit values (which take account of any reduction in exposure provided by hearing protection) must not be exceeded

250 Removing and repairing body panels using pneumatic tools can be noisy work: air saws and chisels (see Figure 69) can typically produce levels as high as 107 dB(A) and grinders and orbital sanders 97 dB(A). Noise levels from panel beating and other repair operations using handtools are variable but generally high; noise from work with sheet metal is often around 93 dB(A). Welding and flamecutting can also be noisy, and paint spraying has been measured at 93 dB(A).

251 HSE's online exposure calculator (www.hse.gov.uk/noise/dailycalc.xls) can be used to estimate if any employee's exposure is likely be at or above 80 dB(A) throughout the day. If it is, then an assessment needs to be carried out by a competent person. When exposure exceeds 85 dB(A), you will have to take increased action to eliminate and/or control exposure.

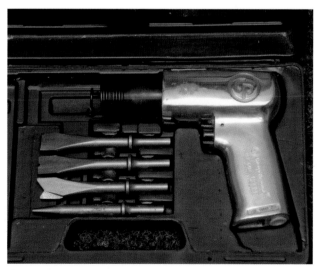

Figure 69 An air chisel produces very high noise and vibration levels

252 The 80 dB(A) and 85 dB(A) exposure action values are likely to be exceeded where bodywork is a regular daily activity and where pneumatic tools are used even for short periods. Using an air saw to remove panels for as little as six minutes can mean the user's total daily personal noise exposure will exceed 85 dB(A). Using an air sander for 45 minutes can give the user a daily personal noise exposure of more than 90 dB(A), as well as causing significant exposure to others nearby.

Selection and use of hearing protection

253 Employers should provide hearing protection that at least reduces noise exposure to below 85 dB(A), but reducing the level of noise to below 70 dB(A) at the ear should be avoided. Check this using the manufacturer's performance data and HSE's online hearing protection calculator (www.hse.gov.uk/noise/hearingcalc.xls).

254 In particular, employers should:

- provide employees with hearing protectors, if they ask for them and their noise exposure is between the lower and upper exposure action values;
- provide employees with hearing protectors and make sure they use them properly when their noise exposure exceeds the upper exposure action values;
- identify hearing protection zones, ie areas where the use of hearing protection is compulsory, and mark them with signs if possible;
- provide employees with training and information on how to use and care for the hearing protectors;
- ensure that the hearing protectors are properly used and maintained.

255 When selecting hearing protection, here are some do's and don'ts:

Do:

- target the use of protectors to the noisy tasks and jobs in a working day;
- select protectors which are suitable for the working environment – consider how comfortable and hygienic they are;
- think about how they will be worn with other protective equipment (eg dust masks and eye protection);
- provide a range of protectors so employees can choose ones which suit them.

Don't:

- provide protectors which cut out too much noise – this can cause isolation, a loss of perception of surrounding events in busy workshops or lead to an unwillingness to wear them;
- make the use of hearing protectors compulsory where the law doesn't require it;
- have a 'blanket' approach to hearing protection – better to target its use and only encourage people to wear it when they need to.

Controlling workplace noise

256 To control workplace noise you need to:

- get suppliers of machinery and equipment to specify noise levels at operators' positions;
- choose quieter machines and/or equipment, eg dampened grinding discs, silenced air compressors and enclosures, silenced air tools etc;
- isolate bodywork repairs in a mobile PVC strip curtain enclosure and/or in separate rooms etc;
- use industry good practice to reduce workplace noise, eg using magnetic mats, sandbags, bracing bodywork etc when body prepping.

Providing health surveillance

257 You must provide health surveillance (audiometric hearing checks) for employees who are likely to be regularly exposed above the upper exposure action values, or are at particular risk, eg they already suffer from hearing loss and/or are particularly sensitive to damage.

258 Health surveillance for hearing damage usually means:

- regular hearing checks in controlled conditions by someone who has the appropriate training;
- telling employees about the results of their hearing checks;
- keeping health records;
- ensuring employees are examined by a doctor where hearing damage is identified.

For further information, see *Controlling noise at work. The Control of Noise at Work Regulations 2005. Guidance on Regulations.*[27]

Vibration exposure

259 Hand-arm vibration is vibration transmitted from work processes into workers' hands and arms. It can be caused by operating hand-held power tools, such as grinders, sanders, impact wrenches and air chisels, which are commonly used in MVR.

260 Regular and frequent exposure to hand-arm vibration can lead to permanent health effects. This is most likely when contact with a vibrating tool or work process is a regular part of a person's job. Occasional and/or infrequent low exposure is unlikely to cause ill health.

261 Hand-arm vibration can cause a range of conditions collectively known as hand-arm vibration syndrome (HAVS), as well as specific diseases, such as carpal tunnel syndrome (CTS).

262 The Control of Vibration at Work Regulations[28] place duties on employers and the self-employed to assess and identify measures to eliminate or reduce risks from exposure to hand-arm vibration. The assessment should:

- identify where there might be a risk from vibration and who is likely to be affected;
- contain a reasonable estimate of employees' exposures;
- identify what needs to be done to comply with the law, eg whether vibration control measures are needed and, if so, where and what type;

- identify any employees who need to be provided with health surveillance and whether any are at particular risk.

263 Advice on carrying out these tasks is given on HSE's hand-arm vibration web pages, including details of how to interpret manufacturers' data and other tools to estimate exposure (www.hse.gov.uk/vibration/hav/index.htm).

264 Identifying signs and symptoms at an early stage is important and employees need to report these to their employer. Symptoms include any combination of:

- tingling and numbness in the fingers;
- not being able to feel things properly;
- loss of strength in the hands;
- fingers going white (blanching) and becoming red and painful on recovery (particularly in the cold and wet, and probably only in the fingertips at first).

265 For some people, symptoms may appear after only a few months of exposure, but for others they may take a few years. They are likely to get worse with continued exposure to vibration and may become permanent. The effects on people include:

- pain, distress and sleep disturbance;
- inability to do fine work (eg assembling small components) or everyday tasks (eg fastening buttons);
- reduced ability to work in cold or damp conditions (ie most outdoor work) which would trigger painful, finger-blanching attacks;
- reduced grip strength, which might affect the ability to do work safely.

Reducing the risks of vibration exposure:

- Use an alternative method of work that reduces vibration.
- Consider purchasing handtools that are vibration reduced.
- Keep handtools in a good state of repair, ie regularly serviced and maintained.
- Keep consumables in balance, ie providing training to eliminate bad tool use.
- Encourage employees to report early symptoms.

For further information see: *Hand-arm vibration. The Control of Vibration at Work Regulations 2005,*[28] and *Hand-arm vibration. Advice for employees.*[29]

Fire and explosion

266 Fires and explosions are major causes of deaths and property damage in MVR. Usually, they involve the mishandling of petrol, eg when draining fuel tanks and lines, but incidents have also occurred during 'hot work' repairs on vehicle diesel tanks and waste-oil storage tanks, during the inappropriate use of paints/thinners/waste petrol to light rubbish fires, and the collection and use of waste engine oil in space heaters.

267 The safe storage and use of all flammable substances are covered by the Dangerous Substances and Explosive Atmospheres Regulations 2002 (DSEAR).[30] Storage of petrol and petroleum products in a workplace no longer requires a licence from the Petroleum Licensing Authority, except for storage of petrol for dispensing into vehicles.

268 DSEAR requires employers to:

■ find out what dangerous substances are in their workplace and what the fire and explosion risks are;

■ put control measures in place to either remove those risks or, where this is not possible, control them;

■ put controls in place to reduce the effects of any incidents involving dangerous substances;

■ prepare plans and procedures to deal with accidents, incidents and emergencies involving dangerous substances;

■ make sure employees are properly informed about and trained to control or deal with the risks from dangerous substances;

■ identify and classify areas of the workplace where explosive atmospheres may occur and avoid ignition sources (eg from unprotected equipment) in those areas.

269 Typical examples of dangerous substances in MVR are shown in Table 4.

270 An explosive atmosphere can be produced by an accumulation of gas, mist, dust or vapour which, when mixed with air, has the potential to catch fire or explode.

271 A number of measures can be taken to eliminate or reduce risks from explosive atmospheres. These include substitution, control measures and mitigation methods.

Table 4 Dangerous substances in MVR

Substance	Where found in MVR
Petrol	Storage/handling in drums/cans, eg from draining fuel tanks/lines, and when working on vehicles
Waste engine oil (particularly if contaminated with petrol)	Storage in drums/tanks and/or use in space heaters
Other flammable liquids	Storage/use of paints, solvents, cleaning materials
Flammable gases	Welding/cutting equipment, LPG heaters, battery charging, LPG-fuelled vehicles, some aerosols
Explosive dusts	Sanding organic fillers, eg fibreglass
Other explosive materials	Airbags, seat belt pretensioners
Flammable materials in special circumstances	Welding/cutting of diesel tanks, or near to brake lines etc

Substitution

272 While there is no scope for substituting petrol or other vehicle fuel, it may be possible to replace paints, solvents or cleaning materials classified as dangerous with ones that are less hazardous, eg using a higher flashpoint solvent or water-based materials. Where risk cannot be entirely eliminated, appropriate control and mitigation measures must be put in place.

Control measures

273 Control measures reduce the probability of an incident occurring. In order of priority, adopt the control measures in Table 5 where reasonably practicable.

Table 5 Control measures – do's and don'ts

Reduce the quantity of dangerous substance to a minimum	**Do** keep stored quantities of petrol and (highly) flammable paints, thinners and solvents, including waste solvents, as low as possible
	Do keep numbers of gas cylinders to a minimum
Avoid or minimise releases	**Do** use a proprietary fuel retriever/adaptor when emptying petrol tanks and pipelines
	Do keep tops/lids on containers of (highly) flammable substances
	Do use safety containers where appropriate
	Do use a proprietary paint mixing system
	Don't spray (highly) flammable paints outside ventilated booth/room
Control releases at source	**Do** use tools with built-in extraction or local exhaust equipment when sanding organic body fillers
	Do ensure that the booth/room extraction is switched on before spraying
Prevent the formation of an explosive atmosphere	**Do** potentially dangerous work in safe and well-ventilated areas, eg in the open air
	Don't drain petrol tanks or pipelines over, or close to, an inspection pit or drain
	Don't carry out welding or other hot work on diesel tanks (unless they have been adequately cleaned and gas freed), or near to fuel tanks/lines, brake lines or inflated tyres
	Don't attempt to repair an LPG fuel tank – seek specialist advice
Collect, contain and remove any releases to a safe place	**Do** maintain extraction/filtration equipment and ensure it is adequate for removing dangerous mists/vapours
	Do dispose of contaminated cloths/rags safely
Avoid ignition sources	**Do** ensure that equipment provided for inspection pits, spray booths and other zoned areas is suitable for use in explosive atmospheres*
	Don't smoke, weld or carry out other hot work while removing petrol or where (highly) flammable vapours could be present
Avoid adverse conditions which could lead to danger	**Do** ensure that temperature controls on drying/curing ovens are properly maintained
	Do keep airbags in properly secured containers
	Don't charge batteries at rates above manufacturers' recommendations
Keep incompatible substances apart	**Don't** store oxygen and flammable gas cylinders together

*The Equipment and Protective Systems Intended for Use in Potentially Explosive Atmospheres Regulations 1996 (SI 1996/192)[31]

Mitigation methods

274 Provide reasonably practicable measures to lessen (mitigate) the effects of any fire, explosion or similar event, including those listed in Table 6.

Hazardous area classification

275 The hazardous area classification of MVR premises is not simple. However, while transient activities involving flammable substances (eg use of aerosols) can take place anywhere on site, the following are examples of places that would normally be considered to be **hazardous:**

- areas for storing, mixing or spraying flammable liquids;
- body preparation areas where organic body fillers are sanded;
- battery charging areas;
- vehicle inspection pits.

276 The special precautions that apply to hazardous places are:

- area classification (zoning):
- selection of equipment (protection from sources of ignition);
- marking of entry points into zones;
- provision of anti-static clothing, if deemed necessary by the risk assessment;
- verification of the safety of plant, processes and equipment before they are brought into use.

Area classification (zoning)

277 Hazardous places are classified in terms of zones on the basis of the likelihood and duration of an explosive atmosphere (the figures 0, 1 and 2 apply to gases, vapours and mists; 20, 21 and 22 to dusts):

- Zone 0/20 – present continuously/for long periods/frequently;
- Zone 1/21 – is likely to occur in normal operation, but only occasionally;
- Zone 2/22 – is not likely to occur normally/for short periods only.

Selection of equipment (protection from sources of ignition)

278 Both electrical and mechanical equipment used in the zones must meet the requirements of the Equipment and Protective Systems Intended for Use in Potentially Explosive Atmospheres Regulations 1996 (EPS).[31] However, if the equipment was in use before July 2003 you can continue to use it, provided the risk assessment shows it is safe to do so and it is maintained in good condition. The following equipment categories apply to the zones:

- Zone 0/20 – Category 1 equipment;
- Zone 1/21 – Category 1 or 2 equipment;
- Zone 2/22 – Category 1, 2 or 3 equipment.

279 Examples of equipment in MVR that might need protection include lighting (fixed and portable, including low-voltage or battery-operated), hand-held drills, grinders, polishers etc, paint spray equipment and drying lamps.

Table 6 Mitigating the effects of fire, explosion etc

Preventing fires and explosions from spreading to other parts of the workplace	**Do** store petrol, paints, solvents and gas cylinders in safe places in the open air if possible, or in storerooms which are in safe positions or are fire-resisting structures
	Do provide at least half-hour, fire-resistant isolation for spray booths/rooms and any storage area inside occupied buildings
Minimising the numbers of workers/ other people who may be at risk	**Do** provide adequate and safe means of escape in case of fire
	Don't allow unauthorised people into zoned areas, eg spray booths/rooms or inspection pits
Providing plant and equipment that can safely contain or suppress an explosion, or vent it to a safe place	**Do** provide and maintain explosion-relief panels where required, eg on dust collection plant or direct-fired drying/curing ovens working at temperatures over 80 °C, and on some ovens in which the air is recirculated. They should be easy to lift, eg by hand pressure

Marking of entry points into zones

280 'Ex' warning signs should be displayed at the entrances to zoned areas, for example flammable stores and spray booths. Supplementary signs may be used to help highlight the risk.

Providing anti-static clothing

281 Employees who work in zoned areas should be provided with appropriate clothing that does not create a risk of an electrostatic discharge igniting an explosive atmosphere.

Verification of safety before coming into use

282 All areas where hazardous explosive atmospheres may be present, and have come into use for the first time after 30 June 2003, must be confirmed as being safe (verified) by a person (or organisation) competent in the field of explosion protection.

Emergency arrangements

283 Emergency arrangements, proportionate to the level of risk, should be prepared where the risk assessment concludes that an accident, incident or emergency could arise, eg a fire or significant spillage, because of the quantity of dangerous substance present. For example:

■ suitable warning (including visual and audible alarms) and communication systems;

■ escape facilities (see Figure 70);
■ emergency procedures;
■ equipment and clothing for essential personnel dealing with the incident;
■ practice drills;
■ information on emergency procedures should be given to employees and the emergency services advised that the information is available.

More advice on emergency arrangements etc can be found in paragraphs 445-446 and in various HSE publications.[21, 32-41]

Safe use of petrol

284 Petrol forms a highly flammable vapour that is easily ignited. Even low-voltage inspection lamps (if damaged) and static electricity (eg generated when petrol flows through pipework and into containers) can cause ignition. Vapour will arise from evaporation of spillages or from a petrol container as it is filled. Small leaks or spills of petrol can escalate into a major incident with fatal or major injuries and extensive property damage (one litre of spilt petrol can produce up to 15 000 litres of a flammable gas mixture).

285 Most petrol spillages and fires directly associated with vehicle fuel systems occur during fuel draining operations rather than repair work on the fuel system itself. Removal of petrol from all or part of the fuel system is often required to carry out repairs on it or possibly other mechanical or bodywork repairs. The risk also arises during the removal of contaminated fuel from tanks following misfuelling, eg where a diesel vehicle has been filled with petrol and vice versa.

Figure 70 Keep emergency exits well signposted and clear of obstructions

It is estimated that misfuelling happens over 120 000 times a year, often requiring fuel draining and replacement. This may be carried out off-site using specially adapted fuel-recovery vehicles. Alternatively, vehicles may be transported to fixed sites for repair.

Fuel retrievers

286 Using a proprietary fuel retriever correctly will eliminate spillage, minimise escaping petrol vapour and provide a suitable and stable container to collect petrol in. The petrol can then be transferred back to the vehicle or to another suitable container (eg a United Nations approved container for the carriage of petrol) for disposal or storage. Proprietary fuel retrievers use earthing straps to eliminate dangerous static discharge and some have vapour recovery pipework (see Figure 71).

287 Fuel retrievers can and should be used in most circumstances when transferring petrol:

■ always work outdoors or in well-ventilated areas, well away from pits or other openings in the ground;

■ follow the manufacturer's instructions, paying particular attention to the correct use of vapour recovery pipework;

■ ensure the vehicle chassis and the retriever are both earthed;

■ ensure that other sources of ignition have been excluded (including disconnecting the vehicle battery);

■ alert other people that fuel draining is taking place, eg by using signs.

Figure 71 Fuel retriever – note metal collection tank and earthing straps

288 Where rollover or anti-siphon devices are fitted, use the appropriate fuel line connector, following the supplier's and vehicle manufacturer's advice. In exceptional circumstances it may be necessary to gain access by removing the tank sender unit. If this is located on the side of the tank, do not try to remove it, unless you are sure the fuel level is below the level of the sender unit.

Draining without a fuel retriever

289 Draining petrol without a retriever is particularly hazardous – only do this as a last resort. A hand-operated siphon or independent manual pump (ie not electrically operated) may be acceptable, provided that transfer pipework is securely positioned at both ends and the vehicle chassis and container are grounded by earthing straps. Following the precautions given for fuel retrievers, petrol should be drained into a suitable metal container large enough to hold the contents of the fuel tank, which can be securely closed after use. The container should have the appropriate hazard labels to show its contents and be stable or held within a stable framework so it can't be easily knocked over.

Other precautions

290 Only a competent person who has been shown how to use the equipment and understands the hazards of the operation should carry out fuel removal. Keep a foam or dry-powder fire extinguisher nearby and ensure operators are trained in its use.

291 Don't dispose of unwanted petrol by adding it to the waste oil tank, or by burning it – any contaminated petrol or petrol/diesel mixtures should be consigned to waste, giving a clear description of the nature of the material.

292 Don't store drained or contaminated fuel in the workplace unless it is to be returned to the vehicle immediately. Store fuel retrievers or containers in a clearly designated area in the workshop, from which ignition sources and combustible materials are excluded. It should not be kept on an escape route and a suitable fire extinguisher should be close at hand. At the end of the working day, move the fuel retriever or petrol container to a petrol or flammable liquids store.

293 Soak up any spills immediately, using absorbent granules or similar material, and dispose of the material safely.

Flamecutting and welding

294 Flamecutting and welding equipment is used in various MVR activities, including removing or repairing components and releasing seized parts. Hazards arise from:

- misuse of welding gear and using the wrong equipment for the job;
- direct contact with heat generated;
- fires caused by the ignition of flammable material on or near cars such as trim, carpets and upholstery and petrol in tanks, fuel lines and nearby containers – often started by sparks or drips of molten metal;
- the storage of gas bottles (especially in the event of a fire);
- hot work on or near containers/pipework that contain or previously contained combustible material; and
- harmful fumes and gases generated during hot work, including those from primer and paint layers, and other surface treatments, such as underseal and galvanized coatings.

295 Many of these hazards may be particularly difficult to avoid or prevent when working inside or underneath vehicles.

Arc welding

296 Severe and sometimes fatal electric shocks happen at electric welding apparatus, whether single or three-phase. At all installations:

- provide fuse protection and mechanically interlock the switch fuse or isolator with the socket outlet, so the plug cannot be inserted or withdrawn with the switch in the 'on' position;
- earth the workpiece to protect the operator if there is an interwinding fault between the primary and secondary windings of the transformer. A robust flexible cable, terminating in a clamp connected to the workpiece and with its other end attached to the metalwork or earth terminal of the power source, is an efficient means of earthing;
- during MIG (metal inert gas) or similar welding, prevent contact between the electrode wire and any earthed metalwork to avoid heavy welding current flowing through the earth continuity conductor and destroying it. Use a safe design such as an insulated spool in an insulated

chamber in the power source with the wire being fed, through insulated rollers and a tube inside the welding cable, to the torch;
- use an insulated box or hook to rest the electrode holder, not the face shield, clothing or rags; and
- maintain the electrode holder welding current return cables, clamps and safety earths in good condition.

297 When welding, wear appropriate clothing that covers arms and legs, and use suitable gloves. Wear goggles when chipping slag or wire-brushing welds.

298 Prevent exposure to direct and reflected ultraviolet (UV) light and infrared rays by wearing protective clothing, and using welding screens. If possible, use dark-coloured wall coating to reduce reflections.

299 Eye protection for welding should be to EN 175:1997 *Personal protection. Equipment for eye and face protection during welding and allied processes*[42] used in conjunction with an appropriate welding filter (EN 169:2002 *Personal eye protection. Filters for welding and related techniques*[43] or EN 379:2003 *Personal eye protection. Automatic welding filters*)[44] to prevent arc eye.

Controlling fumes and gases

300 Use local exhaust ventilation wherever possible and always in confined locations. Mobile extraction units with flexible exhaust hoods and trunking can remove fumes and gases from most locations. Have local exhaust ventilation examined and tested by a competent person every 14 months. Where there is no extraction make sure there is a free flow of air to disperse fumes.

Preventing fires and explosions

301 Never apply heat to containers, tanks or drums that may contain flammable residues. This can result in fatal explosions. Either use cold, non-sparking methods or clean them and make them gas-free first.

302 Remove adjacent flammable trim and upholstery before carrying out hot work, especially where molten metal or sparks may fall onto them. Check that fuel lines and tanks will not be affected; empty and remove any which are near or shield them.

303 Check that body cavities next to welding or flamecutting are not filled with plastic foam, which may be easily ignited. Remove this where necessary and use a heat shield to protect adjacent areas.

Resistance ('spot') welding

304 Spot welding tends to be a more controlled process and produces much less fume and splatter and negligible UV. Eye protection is only required to safeguard against splatter and good general ventilation is usually sufficient.

305 All portable welding guns should have suitable counterbalanced devices for supporting the guns, including cables, unless the design of the equipment makes counterbalancing unnecessary.

Safeguards for flammable gas cylinders

306 Gas cylinders are a convenient way to transport and store gases under pressure but they have a number of hazards, including:

- blast of a gas cylinder explosion or rapid release of compressed gas;
- impact from parts of gas cylinders or valves that fail, or any flying debris;
- contact with the released gas or fluid;
- fire resulting from the escape of flammable gases or fluids (such as LPG);
- impact from falling cylinders; and
- manual handling injuries.

307 To reduce the risk of an accident:

- use propane in preference to acetylene where possible;
- store full and empty cylinders in a safe, well-ventilated place, preferably outside buildings and away from bulk oil storage tanks or anything similar;
- never keep cylinders below ground level, or next to drains, basements and other low-lying places – heavy gases will not disperse easily. Do not leave charged hoses for extended periods where ventilation is poor;
- store gas cylinders that contain liquid (for example acetylene, propane and butane) with their valves uppermost;
- protect cylinders from damage, for example by chaining unstable cylinders in racks, and providing suitable trolleys with restraining chains for moving oxyacetylene sets and other cylinders;
- change cylinders away from sources of ignition in a well-ventilated place;
- minimise damage by using the correct hoses, clamps, couplers and regulators for the particular gas and appliance being used;
- don't leave hoses unprotected where they may be damaged, for example across traffic routes;
- ensure the equipment is checked by a competent person before use. Examine flexible gas and oxygen hoses and replace them if they are damaged or perished – never repair hoses with tape. Inspect gauges and replace any defective gauge or broken glasses. Where equipment is deemed unserviceable, make sure it is withdrawn and clearly identified as not for use;
- never apply grease, oil or other lubricants to oxygen fittings;
- decommission at the end of each day's work – turn off cylinder valves, vent the lines, and then turn off the valves at the blowpipe;
- only allow trained, competent people to use the plant. Minimise the risk of welding flame 'flashback' into hoses or cylinders by training operators in correct lighting-up and working procedures and by fitting flashback arresters onto the regulator, on both the fuel and oxygen supply. Arresters may be fitted on the blowpipe, but these do not give protection from a fire starting in the hose. For long lengths of hose, you should fit arresters on both the blowpipe and the regulator (see Figure 72);
- check any acetylene cylinder which has been involved in a flashback or may have been affected by fire or flames. If it becomes warm or starts to vibrate, evacuate the building immediately and call the emergency fire services;
- use leak-testing fluid to test for leaks – never a flame;
- where flammable gas cylinders are transported for roadside or on-site repair, they should be transported in a well-ventilated (preferably open-topped) vehicle, secured in an upright position, and with the cylinder valves and the valves at the blowpipe turned off.

Figure 72 Oxyacetylene equipment with flashback arresters on the blowpipe and regulator

Manual handling

308 MVR will often require moving heavy or awkwardly shaped objects. Moving such loads (including lifting, lowering, pushing, pulling or carrying) causes over 30% of all injuries in the industry. Musculoskeletal disorders (MSDs) can also happen outside the work environment and then can be made worse by work.

309 MSDs can be caused by a single event, such as a single lift of a heavy object. However, repetitive handling of small loads while in an awkward posture can also lead to an accumulation of injury, causing chronic pain. Whatever their cause, MSDs can impair ability to work at normal capacity. Not all MSDs are preventable but it makes sense to do what you can to stop workers being ill and off work; early reporting of symptoms, proper treatment and suitable rehabilitation are essential.

310 The Manual Handling Operations Regulations 1992[13] require employers and the self-employed to:

■ avoid the need for hazardous manual handling, so far as is reasonably practicable;
■ assess the risk of injury from any hazardous manual handling that cannot be avoided; and
■ reduce the risk of injury from hazardous manual handling, so far as is reasonably practicable.

311 When doing risk assessments, it is important to consult and involve the workforce. Employees and their representatives often know first-hand what the risks in the workplace are and may be able to offer practical solutions to controlling them.

312 The manual handling assessment charts (MAC) are a tool designed to help assess the most common risk factors in lifting (and lowering), carrying and team handling operations. The MAC tool may be useful to identify high-risk manual handling operations and help in the completion of risk assessments. Online training in using the MAC tool can be found at: www.hse.gov.uk/msd/mac.

313 Where possible, use mechanical aids for heavy/awkward items and equipment, for example:

■ Use an engine hoist for removing or replacing vehicle engines and a scissor table for lowering or replacing gearboxes.
■ A powered conveyor will move tyres or other heavy items between levels quickly and safely and eliminates the need to carry tyres on stairs or ladders. For heavy tyres or intensive use, vertical hoists are available (see Figure 73).
■ Handling aids can avoid the need to repeatedly carry items such as exhausts and tyres and reduce the handling-related injury risks. Sack barrows are useful (see Figure 74), especially if stacking tyres 'polo' style. These protect the back and allow more tyres to be moved safely at once.

Figure 73 Vertical hoist used for lifting tyres to mezzanine storage (photograph courtesy of Penny Hydraulics Ltd)

Figure 74 Using a sack barrow

- Three-sided roll cages (see Figure 75) or trolleys are useful, especially when handling into racking. Delivery of tyres and other components in roll cages can mean the difference between repetitive unloading and carrying individual items, and a single trip pushing the roll cage.
- A tyre/wheel trolley or powered pedestrian-operated truck can help move large tyres.
- Tyre changers are available with integrated lifts to mechanically raise the wheel from ground level (see Figure 37).
- Choose delivery vehicles and fitting vehicles with a low and level load floor. Make sure you can fit handling aids, such as ramps, that can stay in the vehicle and be used away from the depot. A ramp with a slope of 30 degrees or less is recommended. For particularly heavy items such as commercial, agricultural or earth-moving equipment tyres, use side or tail lifts (see Figure 76). Avoid raising the heaviest tyres from the floor to the vertical – fit the tyre without removing the wheel from the vehicle where possible.
- A lifting aid for replacing windscreens (see Figure 46) will allow accurate positioning with reduced effort.
- A cylinder trolley for transporting gas cylinders (see Figure 72) and a drum trolley for moving oil drums not only reduces effort, but keeps the load secure.

- Choose a welding set that is best suited to the work undertaken and will reduce the risk of strains and sprains (see the HSE leaflet *Choosing a welding set?*).[34]

314 Employees will need training to use equipment safely, particularly when it is first introduced. Remember to keep handling aids well maintained and sensibly loaded, so they work efficiently and safely.

315 When storing in racking, keep heavier items at ground level. Workers can then roll or lift them out at around waist/chest level. Only the lighter items should be stored above shoulder level, ie those under 10 kg.

316 Training in handling techniques should never be relied on as a way of overcoming deficiencies such as unsuitable loads, bad working conditions or a lack of handling aids.

Figure 75 A three-sided roll cage

Figure 76 Van fitted with wheel lift

Electrical safety

317 The use of electricity in MVR is subject to the Electricity at Work Regulations 1989.[45] The three main hazards from electricity are contact with live parts, fire and explosion. Each year in the UK there are around 1000 incidents at work involving electric shock and/or burns, around 25 of these are fatal. Fires started by poor electrical installations and/or faulty electrical equipment can cause many other deaths and injuries. Electrical equipment igniting flammable vapours can cause explosions.

Fixed electrical installations

318 Ensure that any equipment used on the premises is designed for the environment it is used in and is suitably protected. There are specific standards for electrical equipment for use in potentially explosive atmospheres (see BS EN 60079 series *Electrical apparatus for explosive gas atmospheres*).[46]

319 The fixed electrical installation should be installed by a competent electrician to an appropriate standard such as BS 7671:2008 *Requirements for Electrical Installations*[47] – also known as the IEE Wiring Regulations 17th edition). It should also be properly maintained, which includes inspecting and testing by a competent electrician on a regular basis. Formal testing of the fixed installation should be carried out every three years (see IEE Guidance Note 3 on Inspection and Testing).[48]

320 Ensure switchgear is located where it won't be damaged but is readily accessible and unobstructed for inspection and maintenance. There should be enough fuses or circuit breakers to control supplies to distribution boards and individual circuits. These should be clearly labelled to show the circuit or function controlled.

321 Covers of switchboards and distribution boards should be kept securely closed, as in Figure 77.

322 The electrical wiring should be protected against mechanical damage, preferably by using PVC-insulated wires in steel conduit and/or trunking, or armoured cable with an outer PVC sheath. Plastic-covered, mineral-insulated cable may also be used.

323 In workshops, all parts of the fixed electrical installation should be at least a metre above floor level – to reduce the risk of igniting spilt petrol or flammable liquids.

324 There should be enough socket outlets provided on stanchions and walls above bench level to reduce the number and length of trailing leads.

325 Sockets for equipment in wet or damp environments must be suitably rated for these locations (eg at least IP54 or preferably heavy-duty hose-proof IP57) and further protected by a residual current device (RCD) of 30 mA/40 ms specification or an earth-monitoring device in the electrical supply to the device (see Figure 78). The RCD must be trip-tested at appropriate intervals.

Figure 78 RCD protection provided for portable vacuum cleaner

Figure 77 Secured and labelled switchboard

326 Each item supplied via a permanent cable should have its own switch suitable for electrical disconnection and isolation from the electrical supply. This switch should always be used to disconnect the machine before cleaning and maintenance work.

Portable electrical equipment

327 Portable 230 volt tools, handlamps and their plugs, sockets and flexible leads are often sources of electric shock and burn accidents, some of which are fatal. Air-operated or rechargeable battery-operated handtools do not pose a risk of electric shock and may be a safer alternative. However, the equipment must be suitable for the environment it is used in and this includes areas with potentially explosive atmospheres (eg inspection pits, paint stores etc).

328 Industrial-type plugs and sockets to the appropriate standard (BS EN 60309 series)[49] should ideally be used (see Figure 79).

Figure 79 Industrial-type sockets

329 Extension leads should be flexible – never use semi-rigid cable (eg 'twin and earth'). Neoprene-covered cable resists damage from oil. Extension leads with 13-amp fittings should always have an earth wire.

330 In general, damaged cables should be replaced, not repaired.

331 Electric portable tools should preferably be operated by 110 volts supplied from socket outlets suitably located and fed from a transformer, with the 110-volt secondary output winding centre-tapped to earth, so that the maximum possible shock voltage to earth is 55 volts.

332 'Double-insulated' or 'all-insulated' tools are a valuable precaution against electric shock where a 230-volt supply to portable tools has to be used. However, these are not suitable for wet environments.

333 Low-voltage or battery-operated equipment offers no additional protection against the risk of flammable vapours being ignited by electrical equipment.

334 Cost-effective maintenance of portable electric equipment can be achieved by a combination of:

- visual checks by the user;
- formal visual inspections by a person trained and appointed to carry them out;
- combined inspection and tests by an electrically competent person.

335 Management should follow up these procedures by monitoring the effectiveness of the system and taking action where faults are found. Keep records of inspection and maintenance, noting dates of inspections and remedial work carried out. Portable appliance testing (PAT) should typically be carried out every 6–12 months (see HSE's guidance *Maintaining portable and transportable electrical equipment*).[50]

Handlamps

336 Battery-operated LED or halogen hand/head lamps, as in Figure 80, provide low-voltage alternatives to traditional corded lamps with the additional benefit of having no trailing cable.

Figure 80 Rechargeable LED handlamp

337 Where mains-supplied lamps are required they should either be:

■ 'all insulated'/'double insulated', the bulb protected by a robust cage of insulating material or a transparent insulating enclosure; or
■ supplied by reduced voltages such as 110 volts (centre tapped to earth) and separated extra-low voltage (SELV), which does not exceed 50 volts ac supplied from a double wound transformer giving electrical separation mains input power or 120 volts dc (ripple-free). SELV bulb filaments are heavier and more robust than normal types and are more suited to rough usage.

338 Only totally enclosed hose-proof type handlamps operating at 24 volts or less from a double wound transformer should be used in the wet. Detailed guidance on the safe use of electric handlamps (sometimes referred to as inspection lead lamps) is available in HSE Guidance Note *Selection and use of electric handlamps* (PM38).[51]

339 Vehicle inspection pits, paint storage, preparation, mixing and spraying areas, and places where spilt petrol or LPG could accumulate (eg pits, drains or sumps) are all areas where potentially explosive atmospheres could be present. Handlamps suitable

for use in these environments are available and are specifically constructed for this purpose. The use of low voltage, eg 12 volts, does not give protection against the risk of fires and explosions in potentially explosive atmospheres, unless the handlamp has been constructed in accordance with a suitable method of explosion protection.

Electric storage batteries

340 This section deals with lead/acid batteries used in conventional vehicles, typically 12 or 24 volts. Storage batteries in electrically powered vehicles are covered in paragraphs 349-354.

341 Batteries can store large amounts of energy – they can be dangerous and may explode if used incorrectly, causing chemical burns and wounds from flying fragments. Burns may also occur from metal objects that have become very hot or have exploded after short-circuiting the battery's terminals.

342 The liquid (electrolyte) in lead/acid batteries contains sulphuric acid. This is corrosive, and can permanently damage the eyes and produce serious chemical burns to the skin.

Safe charging

343 Sulphuric acid mist (which can be produced during charging of vented batteries) causes throat irritation and is also believed to cause throat cancer. During charging, hydrogen and oxygen gases are also produced inside a battery, creating an explosive mixture. If this is ignited, the battery may shatter, ejecting sharp fragments and corrosive chemicals.

344 Gases are produced more quickly as the battery gets close to being fully charged. Preferably, use an automated charger, which varies the current supplied according to the charge in the battery. As the battery becomes fully energised, the current drops to a trickle and gassing is greatly reduced. During charging, gas bubbles can become trapped inside the battery. When a vented battery is moved, the trapped gases can be released into the air around the battery, creating the risk of explosion.

345 Valve-regulated ('maintenance-free') batteries are much less likely to release gases, but they still need to be charged carefully. Gas pressure may build up inside the battery if it is charged too quickly or for too long. If this happens, the pressure-relief valves in the battery may open and let the gases escape, again creating an explosion risk.

Using batteries safely

346 Batteries contain a lot of stored energy, which may be released very quickly and unexpectedly, for example if the terminals are bridged (short-circuited) with a conductive object, such as an uninsulated metal spanner, a watch or jewellery etc. This allows a large current to flow through the metal object, making it very hot very quickly (similar to electric arc welding). This can cause serious burns and ignite any explosive gases present around the battery. The sparks can give out enough UV light to damage the eyes.

347 Most vehicle batteries produce quite low voltages, so there is little risk of electric shock. However, some large batteries produce more than 120 volts dc (eg in battery-powered vehicles). In such cases, take measures to protect people from the real danger of electric shock (see paragraphs 349-354).

348 Incorrectly connecting or disconnecting a battery can create sparks that can cause an explosion, particularly if the battery has just been charged and it releases trapped gases. To reduce the risk:

■ turn off all the switches in the circuit. If the battery is in a vehicle, turn off the ignition switch as well; and
■ disconnect the earthed terminal of the battery first.

Electrical safety: vehicles

349 The electrical systems on vehicles can also be a source of electric shock, burn, fire and explosion. In addition to the normal electrical battery ignition circuits, some vehicles are equipped with high-intensity lighting systems and/or are powered as an electric/hybrid vehicle. Each of these systems present additional sources of electrical risk.

350 For high-intensity discharge ('xenon') lighting systems the start-up voltage can be over 20 000 volts, with an operating voltage of around 80 to 90 volts and a frequency of several hundred Hertz (see Figure 81).

351 Electric/hybrid vehicles can have parts of the electrical system operating at 650 volts dc with batteries operating at around 280 volts. Most of these parts of the vehicle will tend not to be serviceable (ie they are replaced rather than repaired). Special precautions may be required for road rescue/recovery and electric/hybrid vehicle manufacturers have produced information for non-dealership personnel and have dealt directly with the emergency services to discuss different rescue scenarios.

Figure 81 Xenon bulb holder

352 Inadvertent contact with the electrical parts of these systems is usually prevented by design (eg by placement, insulation and use of distinct colours). International standards exist for fuel cell vehicles[52] and electric road vehicles[53] to protect people against electric hazards.

353 However, repairs following an accident, fault finding or work on the electrical system may involve access to potentially dangerous electrical systems. As with all electrical work, the person undertaking the work must be competent to do so.

354 The vehicle manufacturer's guidance should be followed. Where possible, no work should be carried out on or near live conductors that may cause danger. For example, safely disconnect the battery before working on high-intensity discharge circuits ('memory keepers' can be used to retain radio codes and other electronic settings).

Mobile steam/water pressure cleaners

355 Mobile steam/water pressure cleaners are commonly used for valeting or cleaning vehicles before examination or repair (see Figure 82). Risks to the operator and others nearby can arise from the electrical supply, from high-pressure jets penetrating the skin, scald injuries from steam, impact injuries from material and debris loosened by the pressure cleaner etc.

General issues

356 If an electrical fault occurs, the wet environment generated can increase the severity of the shock and the likelihood of death or serious injury.

357 Many accidents involving steam/pressure washers have resulted from a fault in the electrical supply/extension cable to the washer. Typically, an earth connection failure had not been detected, and a second wiring fault or insulation failure occurred, allowing exposed conductive parts of the equipment to become live at mains voltage.

358 Pressure washers are usually designed to be used with all exposed metalwork earthed so a fault such as a live conductor touching exposed metalwork will cause the fuse in the supply circuit to blow. It will not be immediately obvious to the user that the earth connection has failed, but this should be detected by routine maintenance (see paragraphs 364-365).

Cables

359 Flexible supply cables should, if possible, be suspended by hooks or other means, and placed where they are least likely to be damaged. Cables may be suspended on a cable bridge, or run through substantial metal pipes secured so they will not be moved by vehicles. Alternatively, armoured cables may be used to protect against mechanical damage.

Plugs and socket outlets

360 Industrial-style plugs and socket outlets which protect against water getting in should normally be

Figure 82 Dedicated area for pressure washing

used. Domestic-style plugs and socket outlets are not suitable for the wet or damp environment around the pressure washer (but it may be possible to site the outlet in a dry, protected area).

361 Equipment that is designed to be drip-proof may be marked IP42. Splash-proof equipment may be marked IP43 and hose-proof equipment may be marked IP55 or IP57.[54]

362 Use residual current protection devices (RCDs) in the supply to the pressure washer. RCDs should be trip-tested before using the washer and subject to regular inspection and testing. The use of adaptor or plug-in type RCD is not recommended because they can be left out of use, or may be unsuitable for wet environments.

363 An alternative to using RCDs is circulating current monitoring. This works by continuously proving the integrity of the earth conductor by circulating a small current through it. A break in this circuit operates the trip mechanism and disconnects the supply. This type of protection is particularly recommended for a vehicle cleaning area.

Maintenance

364 Establish a system of routine maintenance, testing and repair for installations and safety devices, such as that in *Electrical risks from steam/water pressure cleaners*[55] and keep records of examinations, tests and repairs.

365 Instruct and train operators to make external checks (including the operation of the RCD) each day before use and to report defects immediately. Never use an apparently defective machine. In addition to user checks, a competent person should carry out formal visual inspection of the equipment and installation regularly, eg once a week if it is in daily use.

Personal protective equipment

366 Operators may need special clothing to protect them from the liquid used in the cleaner, and the materials on which it is being used. To prevent injection injuries at high-pressure steam/water cleaners, never lock the trigger or foot switch in the 'on' position and consider eye protection to safeguard against eye injuries from flying debris.

367 Further information for operators is given in the HSE leaflet *Do you use a steam/water pressure cleaner? You could be in for a shock!*[56]

Work at height

368 Falls from height are the most common cause of death and serious injury to people at work. They account for nearly 10 per cent of injuries in MVR – mainly involving falls from ladders.

369 The Work at Height Regulations 2005 (WAHR)[57] define work at height as work in any place, including a place at or below ground level (including access and exit routes) where a person could fall a distance liable to cause personal injury. In MVR this will include tall storage racks such as those used for tyre storage, roof areas used for storage (eg mezzanine floors), vehicle inspection pits (see paragraphs 214-232), work on the top of commercial vehicles (eg refrigeration units) and paint spraying of larger vehicles (see Figures 17 and 83).

370 The Regulations set out a hierarchy for managing and selecting equipment for work at height:

■ Can work at height be avoided?
■ Where you must work at height, what can be put in place that would prevent a person falling? Examples of this include mobile or fixed platforms that can be used to access the sides of vehicles (see Figures 84-86), use of guard rails and toe boards.
■ If there is still a risk of falling, what can be done to reduce the distance and consequences of a fall (eg soft landing bags)?

■ What other measures might reduce the risk of injury (eg extra training or competence)?

371 If an upper or mezzanine floor/area is used for storage, make sure it is load bearing, has adequate fencing and there is sufficient head height. Fencing will normally consist of two guard rails with the top rail at least 1100 mm above the decking. Provide an adequate upstand or toe board to prevent objects falling from the edge (see Figure 87).

372 Use a conventional fixed or appropriately secured staircase for access between floors. If a staircase cannot be accommodated, properly secured steps and ladders may be used, provided they are restricted to people who are capable of using them safely and any loads can be carried without undue risk. Where a mechanical lifting device is required, do not exceed the safe working load and only use it for carrying stock – never people.

373 If the lifting device is attached to the mezzanine floor structure it should be installed by a competent person to ensure the structure is capable of supporting both the lifting device and its safe working load. Maintain all lifting devices and have them inspected by a competent person every year. Damaged gates, lift switchgear or equipment should be repaired immediately. Where mechanical lifting devices are not used, only light, easily manageable materials should be stored on upper floors. Ensure that upper floors, particularly mezzanine floors, are not overloaded.

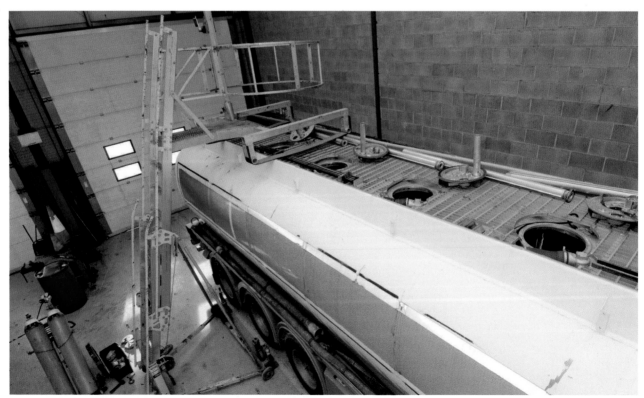

Figure 83 Ladder access and harness provision for working on top of a tanker

It may be necessary to provide a notice stating the safe working load.

374 Guard all openings on upper floors to prevent any goods or people falling. It is particularly important that any sections of the guard which are removable for loading (eg by forklift truck) are replaced as soon as loading is complete. Preferably, use a system of guarding which allows goods to be transferred to and from mezzanine floors while maintaining adequate protection against falls (see Figures 88 and 89). Never allow people to drop or throw items from one floor to another.

375 Where possible, reduce storage rack height as this can significantly reduce the risk.

376 Provide good, stable steps for access to storage racking. These should preferably have handrails and a small platform at the top but need to be practical and easily manoeuvred. Heavier items should be stored on lower racks. Stock should never be retrieved by climbing the racking.

377 Only use ladders for low-risk, short-duration work, or where site conditions (that cannot be changed) dictate. Inspect any access equipment exposed to conditions causing deterioration at suitable intervals and following circumstances where the condition of the equipment could be jeopardised. Ladders used with storage racking should have hooks or other

Figure 84 Mobile platform for vehicle access

Figure 85 Mobile working platform for coaches (photograph courtesy of First Group Plc)

Figure 86 Fixed working platform for buses (photograph courtesy of First Group Plc)

devices that attach to the racking, so the ladder does not move or slide. Apply the 'one in four' ladder rule (one unit out for every four units up) and make sure there is sufficient space between aisles to allow people to exit safely from the ladder.

378 Equipment provided for work at height (such as ladders, guard rails, platforms, toe boards) needs to be inspected at suitable intervals. This should be determined on the basis of risk assessment carried out by a competent person. It should specify the nature, frequency and extent of any inspection by considering factors such as the type of equipment, how and where it is used, how likely it is to deteriorate etc. If equipment is used in outdoor conditions, and is subject to bad weather etc, it may be appropriate to inspect it more regularly than equipment used indoors.

Figure 87 Stable racking with protection against falling objects

Figures 88 and 89 Pivoting safety barrier ensures that the fence opening is guarded at all times

General working conditions

379 The Workplace (Health, Safety and Welfare) Regulations 1992[58] outline an employer's duties to provide a hygienic workplace with ready access to essential welfare facilities for all members of a workforce (including people with disabilities, and pregnant and nursing mothers where applicable).

Ventilation

380 Workplaces need to be adequately ventilated. Fresh, clean air should be drawn from a source outside the workplace, uncontaminated by discharges from flues, chimneys or other process outlets, and be circulated through the workrooms. Windows and vehicle entrances may provide sufficient ventilation but, where necessary, mechanical ventilation systems should be provided and regularly maintained.

Lighting

381 Provide suitable and sufficient lighting to all parts of the premises and not just to the work area. There should be a good level of illumination, free from glare. Position light fittings so light is even throughout the working area and strong shadows are avoided. Remedy all light failures or deficiencies as soon as possible and keep light covers clean. The lighting level needed depends on:

■ how much detail needs to be seen;
■ the speed and accuracy required by the task; and
■ employees' individual needs.

383 For most general MVR tasks, the average luminance for the work area should be at least 100 lux with a minimum of 50 lux at any position in it.

384 Bodyshop lighting levels are much more demanding. Lighting needs to be as uniform as possible and without glare, with an average figure in spray booths of around 1000 lux measured at floor level around a vehicle and between 750 and 1000 lux in preparation areas. Failure to provide and maintain adequate lighting levels in spray booths makes it more likely that sprayers will lift their visors to see the quality of finish (see paragraph 91).

385 Consider wall and floor finishes, for example light colours can improve brightness, whereas darker colours can reduce arc welding flash or reflections from UV lamps.

386 Too much light may cause glare and reduce the amount you can see, as the eye naturally reacts to the brightness.

387 Flickering lamps can cause rotating parts of engines and wheels to appear stationary, so could be dangerous. Flicker can be caused by lamps at the end of their life or by instabilities in the electricity supply. These stroboscopic effects can be eliminated by using lights with high-frequency electronic control gear or by using twin fluorescent lamps with phase displacement between them.

388 Adequate emergency lighting is required, particularly for areas lacking daylight.

389 Ensure that outside areas are satisfactorily lit for work, vehicle movements and other access (particularly during the hours of darkness) – for security as well as safety.

Lighting for specific areas

390 Lights on the runways of vehicle lifts can provide an even and accessible source of illumination. They need to be sufficiently robust and protected against water (see paragraph 325).

391 Lighting used in pits, spray booths, mixing rooms and other areas where flammable atmospheres may be reasonably expected should be designed and tested ('flameproof') or installed to prevent ignition, eg by fitting lights outside the enclosure and shining them through fixed and sealed half-hour, fire-resisting glass (see paragraphs 266-283).

392 In vehicle washes, lights should be totally enclosed and hose-proof.

Indoor workplace temperatures

393 Environmental factors (such as humidity and sources of heat in the workplace) combine with personal factors (such as the clothing a worker is wearing and how physically demanding their work is) to influence 'thermal comfort'.

394 Individual personal preference makes it difficult to specify a thermal environment that satisfies everyone. For workplaces where the activity is mainly sedentary, such as offices, the temperature should normally be at least 16° C. If work involves physical effort it should be at least 13° C.

395 Provide suitable clothing for the job, especially for those working outdoors, in the wet, eg doing vehicle washing or roadside repair or where movement of vehicles in and out of workshops makes it difficult to maintain a suitable temperature in winter.

Toilet and washing facilities

396 Provide suitable and sufficient toilet and washing facilities at readily accessible places. They and the rooms containing them should be kept clean, adequately ventilated and lit. Washing facilities should have running hot and cold or warm water, soap and clean towels or other means of cleaning or drying. Providing dispensers for pre-work ('barrier') creams, cleansers and after-work creams makes it more likely that workers will use them (see Figure 90). Men and women should have separate facilities, unless each facility is in a separate room with a lockable door and is for use by only one person at a time.

Skin care

397 Dermatitis is common in MVR and disease rates are up to seven times the average for UK workers. Symptoms can be so severe that sufferers have to leave the industry.

398 Causes include materials that cause allergy ('sensitisation'), for example chemicals in two-part glues, body fillers and sealants. Many materials can cause dermatitis through irritation or drying out the skin. These include contact with oils, solvents, fuels (including biofuels), ultra-violet radiation and abrasive materials.

399 Some substances used in MVR may affect the skin in other ways. For example, frequent and prolonged contact with used engine oils may lead to other skin disorders, including skin cancer. Contact with battery acid can cause burns.

400 Get information from suppliers' data sheets and tell workers about any substances with risk phrases such as:

- R34 Causes burns;
- R35 Causes severe burns;
- R38 Irritating to skin;
- R43 May cause sensitisation by skin contact;
- R66 Repeated exposure may cause skin dryness or cracking.

401 Check packaging for symbols such as those below but remember that powerful hand cleaners will also remove oil from the skin.

Harmful **(Xn)** Irritant **(Xi)**

Corrosive **(C)** Oxidising agent **(O)**

Figure 90 Clean washing facilities with dispensers for skin care products

402 Manage the problem by adopting the APC approach:

- **A**voiding contact
- **P**rotecting skin
- **C**hecking for early signs of dermatitis

Avoiding contact

403 To avoid contact with the skin, consider:

- automation, eg computerised paint mixing, automated gun cleaning, two-part dispenser/ mixing systems;
- enclosure, eg dedicated areas where contamination may occur with no access to unprotected staff;
- local exhaust ventilation (LEV), to remove sanding material etc;
- housekeeping, prompt clean-up of spills etc.

Protecting skin

404 If contact cannot be completely avoided then skin needs protecting. In MVR this will typically include a combination of the following.

- Choosing the right gloves. Material selection is important; single-use nitrile gloves are commonly used, but if latex ones are required, make sure they are low-protein and non-powdered. Single-use gloves offer little chemical resistance but may be suitable for short-term protection and will keep hands much cleaner. Practise the correct method of removal to avoid spreading contamination (see www.hse.gov.uk/skin/videos/gloves/ removegloves.htm).
- If workers are wearing gloves for extended periods, liners should be used to absorb sweat. Liners can be washed at the end of the day and left to dry overnight in a clean area.
- Promptly remove skin contamination by washing in warm water.
- Use the mildest cleaner that will get the job done.
- Pre-work creams (sometimes misleadingly described as 'barrier creams' as they do not provide a 'barrier' during work) may be useful and can make cleaning the hands much easier.
- After-work creams (moisturisers) help reduce damage and promote repair of the skin. They should be used at the end of each work shift or after hand washing.
- Provide employees with information, instruction and training on the nature of the risks to health and the precautions to take. This should include characteristic signs and symptoms of skin disease.

Checking for early signs of dermatitis

405 Employees should examine their skin for any such signs and report them. Where the requirement for health surveillance has been identified, these reports should be made to the responsible person appointed to undertake the surveillance or to the company's occupational health adviser. Otherwise, employees should report to their family doctor; confidentiality should be safeguarded.

406 A responsible person is someone, appointed by the employer, who (following instruction from a medical practitioner or occupational health nurse) is competent to recognise skin conditions likely to occur. The responsible person reports findings to the employer, but should also have access to a suitably qualified person (eg an occupational health nurse or medical practitioner), to whom all suspected skin problems should be referred.

407 Health surveillance, such as skin checks, will help to identify the early symptoms of dermatitis or other health effects caused by skin exposure. The earlier the health effect is recognised the better the prognosis for the sufferer. Health surveillance can show whether an adequate standard of control is being maintained. More advice on managing hazards to the skin can be found at www.hse.gov.uk/skin.

Drinking water

408 Provide an adequate supply of high-quality drinking water, with an upward drinking jet or suitable cups. Provide water in refillable enclosed containers where it cannot be obtained directly from a mains supply.

Accommodation for clothing and changing facilities

409 Provide sufficient, suitable and secure space to store workers' own clothing and work wear. As far as is reasonably practicable, the facilities should:

- allow for drying clothing;
- be readily accessible from workrooms and washing and eating facilities;
- ensure the privacy of the user; and
- be big enough and contain seating.

Facilities for resting and eating meals

410 Provide suitable and sufficient, readily accessible rest facilities with adequate seating (see Figure 91). Where workers regularly eat meals at work, suitable and sufficient facilities should be provided for the purpose, preferably segregated from the workshop. Work areas can be used as rest areas and as eating facilities, provided they are adequately clean and there is a suitable surface for food.

411 Any eating facility should include provision for preparing or obtaining a hot drink. Where hot food cannot be obtained in or reasonably near to the workplace, workers should be provided with a means for heating their own food (eg a microwave oven).

412 Since 1 July 2007, it has been illegal to smoke in virtually all enclosed public places and workplaces in England, including most work vehicles. Similar legislation exists in Scotland and Wales.

Cleanliness

413 Interior walls and ceilings should be tiled, painted or otherwise treated, so they can be kept clean. Absorbent floors (eg untreated concrete or timber), which are likely to be contaminated with oil or other substances that are difficult to remove, should preferably be sealed or coated. Remove any dirt and refuse that is not in suitable receptacles daily.

Floors and traffic routes

414 'Traffic route' means a route for pedestrian traffic, vehicles, or both, and includes any stairs, fixed ladders, doorways, gateways, loading bays or ramps.

415 There should be an adequate number of traffic routes, of sufficient width and headroom, to allow people and vehicles to circulate safely with ease.

416 To allow people and vehicles to move safely, the best approach is to keep vehicles and pedestrians apart by ensuring they use entirely separate routes. If people and vehicles have to share a traffic route, use kerbs, barriers or clear markings to designate a safe walkway and, where pedestrians need to cross a vehicle route, provide clearly marked crossing points with good visibility, bridges or subways (see Figure 92). Make sure the shared route is well lit.

417 It is often difficult for drivers to see behind their vehicle when they are reversing; as far as possible, plan traffic routes so that drivers do not need to reverse, for example by using one-way systems and drive-through loading areas.

418 Set appropriate speed limits, and make sure they, and any other traffic rules, are obeyed. Provide route markings and signs, so drivers and pedestrians know where to go and what rules apply to their route and so they are warned of any potential hazards (see Figure 93).

419 Floors and traffic routes should be sound and strong enough for the loads placed on them and the traffic expected to use them. The surfaces should not have holes or be uneven or slippery, and should be kept free of obstructions and from any article or substance which may cause a person to slip, trip or fall.

Figure 91 Mess room with storage lockers and collection point for workwear laundry

Figure 92 Pedestrian segregation using designated footpaths

420 Open sides of staircases should be fenced with an upper rail at 900 mm or higher, and a lower rail. A handrail should be provided on at least one side of every staircase, and on both sides if there is a particular risk. Additional handrails may be required down the centre of wide staircases. Access between floors should not be by ladders or steep stairs.

421 Clean floor and indoor traffic routes at least once a week (see Figure 94). Where a leak or spillage presents a slipping hazard, take immediate steps to fence it off, mop it up or cover it with absorbent granules. Make sure procedures are in place to remove silicone and other polishes, and water coming in during wet weather, from tiled floors in showrooms and similar areas that are normally clean and dry.

422 Provide good drainage in wet processes, particularly vehicle washing areas, and suitable footwear or working platforms where necessary. Areas that cannot be kept dry (eg where vehicles are regularly brought in from outside) require precautions to prevent people slipping and vehicles skidding. This may be achieved by fitting non-skid surfaces or improving the existing flooring, eg by chemically treating tiled areas to improve the surface roughness. Where there is still a risk of slipping, special footwear may be necessary.

423 Big improvements have been made in the performance and testing of slip-resistant flooring and footwear. Some footwear standards have been found to give a poor indication of real-life performance. See HSE's slips and trips web pages for details (www.hse. gov.uk/slips).

424 HSE's slips assessment tool is a freely downloadable computer software package that can be used to assess the slip potential of pedestrian walkway surfaces (see www.hsesat.info).

Windows and similar surfaces

425 Windows and transparent or translucent surfaces in walls, partitions, doors and gates should, where necessary, be made of safety material or protected against breakage. If there is a danger of people coming into contact with it, you should mark these clearly or incorporate features to make it apparent.

Doors and gates

426 Doors and gates that swing both ways, and conventionally hinged doors on main traffic routes, should have a transparent viewing panel.

427 Horizontal swinging barriers used as gates at car parks or similar entrances should be locked open or locked shut (preferably by padlock) so they do not swing open and present a risk to oncoming vehicles.

428 Power-operated doors and gates should have safety features to prevent people being struck or trapped. Where necessary, provide a readily identifiable and accessible control switch or device, so they can be stopped quickly in an emergency.

Figure 93 Clear layout of site entrance and marshal for directing traffic

Figure 94 Ensure that floors and traffic routes are cleaned as required

Safety in MVR offices

429 The office environment is generally safer than the workshop but do consider the following issues.

Electrical wiring

430 Ensure there are enough sockets to minimise the use of adapters. Cover trailing leads to prevent damage and reduce tripping hazards. Carry out visual checks on plugs and leads to look for defects. Earthed equipment such as kettles and some vacuum cleaners should have a portable appliance test to cover the item, plug and lead every one to two years.

Use of computers

431 The Health and Safety (Display Screen Equipment) Regulations 2002[59] apply where employees habitually use computer monitors and similar screens as a significant part of their normal work. Those who use them occasionally are only specifically covered by the workstation requirements of the Regulations (but their employers still have general duties to protect them under other health and safety legislation).

432 Employers need to look at:

- the whole workstation, including equipment, furniture, and the work environment (eg lighting and window coverings, to ensure the screen is free from glare and reflections – see Figure 95);
- the job being done; and
- any special needs of individual staff.

433 Employees should be encouraged to take part in risk assessments, eg by reporting health problems. Where risks are identified, the employer must take steps to reduce them.

434 The user needs to be able to:

- adopt a good posture, placing the mouse close so it can be used with a relaxed arm and straight wrist;
- support the arm, for example on the desk surface; and
- take frequent breaks and try to limit the time spent using the mouse.

435 If users still find gripping the mouse awkward, try a different sized or shaped mouse, or another device such as a trackball.

436 Employees covered by the Regulations can ask their employer to provide and pay for an eye and eyesight test. This is a test by an optometrist or doctor. There is also an entitlement to further tests at regular intervals; the optometrist doing the first test can recommend when the next should be. Employers only have to pay for glasses if special ones (for example, prescribed for the distance at which the screen is viewed) are needed and normal ones cannot be used.

Figure 95 Assess DSE workstations

Organising health and safety in MVR: legal duties

437 If you run an MVR or associated business, either as an employer or as a self-employed person, you must ensure, so far as is reasonably practicable, the health and safety of yourself and others who may be affected by what you do or fail to do.

438 You have duties towards people who:

- work for you, including casual workers, part-timers, trainees and subcontractors (if you are an employer);
- use workplaces you provide (if you are a landlord);
- are allowed to use your equipment (if you allow friends to repair their own vehicles on your premises);
- visit your premises (including contractors and members of the public);
- may be affected by your work (your neighbours, the public and other workpeople).

439 You also have a duty to take reasonable care of yourself and to co-operate with others in complying with their duties.

440 Health and safety is about sensible, proportionate actions that protect people – not unnecessary bureaucracy and paperwork. These are some of the key actions required by law that apply to nearly every business.

- Most employers need to take out Employers' Liability Compulsory Insurance and display the certificate.
- Make sure you have someone competent to help you meet your health and safety duties. This does not have to be an external consultant.
- Decide how you are going to manage health and safety. This is your health and safety policy.
- Decide what could harm people and what precautions to take. This is your risk assessment.
- Provide free health and safety training for your workers.
- Display the health and safety law poster or give workers a leaflet with the information. They need to be able to understand it.

- Report some work-related accidents, diseases and dangerous occurrences as required by the Reporting of Injuries, Diseases and Dangerous Occurrences Regulations 1995 (RIDDOR)[60] – see paragraphs 456 to 458.

441 Free health and safety advice for small businesses is given on HSE's 'Looking after your business' web pages (www.hse.gov.uk/business/index.htm).

Carrying out a risk assessment

442 Risk assessment is fundamental to managing health and safety in the workplace; it helps identify the real issues and allows them to be prioritised. Working in a familiar environment can lead to risks being overlooked. The process of risk assessment forces a systematic identification of hazardous situations and substances and makes it less likely that risks will go unnoticed.

443 Don't overcomplicate the process. In many organisations, the risks are well known and the necessary control measures are easy to apply. If you are confident you understand what's involved, you can do the assessment yourself – you don't have to be a health and safety expert. There are example risk assessments for different MVR facilities on HSE's website (www.hse.gov.uk/risk/casestudies) and a blank risk assessment template to guide you.

444 There is no set way to conduct an assessment but it will typically follow the process outlined in the boxed text below (the HSE leaflet *Five steps to risk assessment* gives more information).[61]

Emergency procedures

445 When things go wrong, people may be exposed to serious and immediate danger. Special procedures are necessary in MVR facilities for emergencies such as serious injuries, explosion, electric shock, fire and chemical spills.

446 Write an emergency plan if a major incident at your workplace could involve risks to the public, rescuing employees or the co-ordination of emergency services. Think about:

- the worst that can happen if things go wrong;
- how the person in charge and others will deal with the problems. You should look at any particular responsibilities and training needs;
- whether everyone is adequately prepared and if emergency services could get to the site.

Five steps to risk assessment

STEP 1: What are the hazards?

This publication and HSE's MVR web pages (www.hse.gov.uk/mvr) should help you to identify the hazards. The manufacturers' instructions or data sheets for chemicals and equipment need to be collected and analysed. COSHH essentials sheets can be downloaded from the MVR web pages for a variety of related tasks. A proper assessment cannot be done by sitting in an office or copying someone else's – you need to walk around the premises noting things that might pose a risk.

Talk to staff and listen to their concerns about health and safety and how they think risks can best be controlled. Confirm what training they have been given, and consider any requirements particular individuals may have. Check the accident book to identify what problems have occurred in the past.

STEP 2: Who might be harmed and how?

Write down who could be harmed by the hazards and how – this includes visitors and members of the public.

STEP 3: What are you doing already? What further action is necessary?

For each hazard identified, record what controls, if any, were in place to manage them, and then compare these controls to HSE and industry guidance. Where existing controls do not meet good practice, write down what further actions are needed to manage the risk.

STEP 4: How will you put the assessment into action?

You need to discuss the findings of the risk assessment with your staff. Prioritise and deal with hazards that are high-risk and have serious consequences first. Decide and record who is responsible for implementing the further actions and when they should be done. When each action is complete, tick it off and record the date.

STEP 5: Review date

Decide when to review and update the risk assessment (eg annually and after any major change to work practice).

You may find it useful to use the risk assessment as part of the induction process for new staff.

Points to include in emergency procedures

- Consider what might happen and how the alarm will be raised. Don't forget weekends and (possibly) times when the premises are closed, eg holidays.
- Plan what to do, including how to call the emergency services and help them by clearly marking your premises from the road. Consider drawing up a simple plan marked with the location of hazardous items, eg flammables store, gas bottles etc.
- Decide where to go to reach a place of safety or to get rescue equipment. Provide emergency lighting if necessary.
- You must make sure there are enough emergency exits for everyone to escape quickly, and keep emergency doors and escape routes unobstructed and clearly marked (see Figure 96).
- Nominate competent persons to take control.
- Decide who the other key people are, such as first-aiders (see paragraphs 450-455).
- Plan essential actions such as emergency plant shut-down or making processes safe; clearly label important items like shut-off valves and electrical isolators for plant and machinery.
- Train everyone in emergency procedures.
- Don't forget the needs of people with disabilities.

Figure 96 Keep escape routes unobstructed and clearly marked. Note automatic release for doors in the event of a fire

Investigating events

447 If an accident happens:

- take any action required to deal with the immediate risks, eg put out the fire, isolate any danger, apply first aid, fence off the area;
- assess the amount and kind of investigation needed – if you have to disturb the site, take photographs and measurements first;
- investigate – find out what happened and why;
- take steps to stop something similar happening again;
- also look at near misses and property damage. Often it is only by chance that someone wasn't injured.

448 To help with your investigations, find out the following:

- What are the details of injured people?
- What are the details of injury, damage or loss?
- What was the worst that could have happened? Could it happen again?
- What happened? Where? When? What was the direct cause?
- Were there standards in place for the premises, plant, substances or procedures involved?
- Were they adequate? Were they followed?
- Were the people competent, trained and instructed?
- What was the underlying cause? Was there more than one?
- What was meant to happen and what were the plans? How were the people organised?
- Would inspection have picked up the problem earlier?
- Had it happened before? If so, why weren't the lessons learnt?

449 Most accidents have more than one cause so don't be too quick to blame individuals – try to deal with the root causes.

First aid

450 Immediate and proper examination and treatment of injuries may save life – and is essential to reduce pain and help injured people make a quick recovery. Neglect or incorrect treatment of an apparently trivial injury may lead to infection and ill health. An appropriate level of first-aid treatment should be available in the workplace.

451 Appoint someone to take charge in an emergency, to call an ambulance and to look after the first-aid equipment (see Figure 97). At least one 'appointed person' must be available at all times when people are at work.

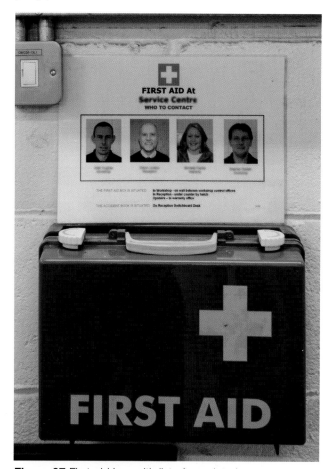

Figure 97 First-aid box with list of appointed persons

452 There is no mandatory list of contents for first-aid boxes; it is based on the employer's assessment of first-aid needs. A suggested minimum stock of items, where there is no special risk in the workplace, would be:

- a leaflet giving general guidance on first aid, eg HSE leaflet *Basic advice on first aid at work*;[62]
- 20 individually wrapped, sterile, adhesive dressings (assorted sizes);
- two sterile eye pads;
- four individually wrapped, triangular bandages (preferably sterile);

- six safety pins;
- six medium-sized (approximately 12 cm x 12 cm), individually wrapped, sterile, unmedicated wound dressings;
- two large (approximately 18 cm x 18 cm), sterile, individually wrapped, unmedicated wound dressings;
- one pair of disposable gloves.

453 Equivalent but different items will be considered acceptable. Safely dispose of any items in the first-aid box that have passed their expiry date. In general, tablets and medication should not be kept in the first-aid box.

454 Display notices giving the locations of first-aid equipment and the name and location of the appointed person or first-aider. In larger repair businesses you may need a first-aid room, a qualified first-aider or someone with specialist first-aid training.

455 In all vehicle repair businesses it makes sense to have someone who knows the basics of first aid, eg resuscitation, control of bleeding, and treatment of an unconscious patient. Make sure your first aid arrangements cover those who work away from their base, such as vehicle recovery operators.

Reporting accidents, incidents and diseases

456 Employers, the self-employed, and anyone in control of work premises have legal duties under the RIDDOR Regulations[60] to record and report some work-related accidents by the quickest means possible. These include:

- deaths;
- major injuries;
- over-three-day injuries – where an employee or self-employed person is unable to perform their normal work for more than three consecutive days;
- injuries to members of the public or people not at work where they are taken from the scene of an accident to hospital;
- some work-related diseases including occupational asthma arising from exposure to isocyanates, hand-arm vibration syndrome, and occupational dermatitis;
- dangerous occurrences (near misses), including the collapse of lifts and hoists, and the escape of any substance in a quantity sufficient to cause death, major injury or damage to health.

457 RIDDOR applies to all work activities but not all incidents are reportable. Call the Incident Contact Centre (ICC) on 0845 300 9923 and they will take details if it is reportable. You can also contact them online at www.hse.gov.uk/riddor. Copies of submitted RIDDOR forms are sent to employers/dutyholders and any errors or omissions can be corrected.

458 Details of all accidents can be kept in an accident book, such as HSE's *Accident book* (BI 510).[63]

Special considerations

459 **Children** below the minimum school leaving age (MSLA) must not be employed in MVR etc except when on work experience schemes approved by the local authority, or the governing body of an independent school. There are also restrictions on the part-time employment of children in other work, such as car washing and working in shops attached to garages. Employers must let the parents/carers of any children below the MSLA know the key findings of the risk assessment and the control measures introduced, before the child starts work or work experience.

460 **Young people** are those aged below 18. As with children, employers must:

- assess risks to all young people, **before** they start work;
- ensure the risk assessment takes into account their psychological or physical immaturity, inexperience, and lack of awareness of existing or potential risks;
- introduce control measures to eliminate or minimise the risks, so far as is reasonably practicable.

461 **New and expectant mothers** may be at greater risk from different physical, biological, and chemical agents, working conditions and processes. These risks will vary depending on their health, and at different stages of their pregnancy. Employers should ensure that workers who are, or in the future could be, new or expectant mothers are not exposed to any significant risk and to inform them of any hazards identified. On receiving written notification of the pregnancy, the employer should carry out a specific risk assessment with the expectant mother, taking into account any advice received from the woman's doctor or midwife. Some of the more common risks might include:

- lifting/carrying heavy loads;
- standing or sitting for long lengths of time;
- exposure to lead;
- work-related stress;
- workstations and posture;
- long working hours; or
- excessively noisy workplaces.

462 Employers have to provide suitable facilities for pregnant and breastfeeding mothers to rest. Where necessary, these should include somewhere for them to lie down.

463 **Members of the public** should be restricted to low risk areas of the premises (which could include clearly marked walkways) or escorted by a member of staff. Where customers are allowed to drive their vehicles into the work area (including onto ramps or over pits), it makes sense to check that they are confident to do so. There should be a safe and clearly defined walkway back to the waiting area.

464 **Safety representatives** may be appointed by a recognised trade union. They can investigate accidents and potential hazards, pursue employee complaints and carry out inspections of the workplace. They are also entitled to certain information and to paid time-off to train for their health and safety role. In workplaces where a union is not recognised, employees must be consulted on health and safety, either directly or through their elected representatives.[64]

Enforcing the law

465 Health and safety laws relating to your firm will be enforced by inspectors from HSE or a health and safety enforcement officer from your local council. They are aware of the special risks of MVR work and will give you help and advice on how to comply with the law. They are legally empowered to:

- visit workplaces without notice, but you are entitled to see their identification before they come in;
- investigate an accident or complaint, or inspect the safety, health and welfare aspects of your business;
- talk to employees and safety representatives, take photographs and samples, and even in certain cases impound dangerous equipment;
- receive co-operation and answers to questions.

466 If there is a problem they may issue a formal notice requiring improvements or, where serious danger exists, a notice that prohibits the use of a process or equipment. For the most serious breaches of health and safety law, they may prosecute a firm or an individual (or report to the Procurator Fiscal with a view to prosecution in Scotland).

References

1   *Work with lubricants and waste oil*
COSHH essentials sheet SR19 HSE 2006
www.hse.gov.uk/pubns/guidance/sr19.pdf

2   *Vehicle exhaust fumes (in warehouses, garages etc)* COSHH essentials sheet SR14 HSE 2006
www.hse.gov.uk/pubns/guidance/sr14.pdf

3   *Simple guide to the Provision and Use of Work Equipment Regulations 1998* Leaflet INDG291
HSE Books 2008 (single copy free or priced packs of 15 ISBN 978 0 7176 2429 4)
www.hse.gov.uk/pubns/indg291.pdf

4   *Asbestos essentials: A task manual for building, maintenance and allied trades on non-licensed asbestos work* HSG210 (Second edition)
HSE Books 2008 ISBN 978 0 7176 6263 0
www.hse.gov.uk/asbestos/essentials

5   *A guide to handling and storage of airbags and seat belt pretensioners at garages and motor vehicle repair shops* Leaflet INDG280 HSE Books 1998 (single copy free or priced packs of 10
ISBN 978 0 7176 1614 5)
www.hse.gov.uk/pubns/indg280.htm

6   *Control of substances hazardous to health (Fifth edition). The Control of Substances Hazardous to Health Regulations 2002 (as amended). Approved Code of Practice and guidance* L5 (Fifth edition)
HSE Books 2005 ISBN 978 0 7176 2981 7

7   *Safe working with vehicle air-conditioning systems: Guidance for employers, self-employed people, and supervisors* Leaflet INDG349 HSE Books 2002 (single copy free or priced packs of 10
ISBN 978 0 7176 2278 8) www.hse.gov.uk/pubns/indg349.pdf

8   *Review of commercially available party fog machines suitable for determining the clearance time of paint spray booths and rooms* Research report HSL/2006/43, free to download from HSE's website: www.hse.gov.uk/research/hsl_pdf/2006/hsl0643.pdf

9   *Biological monitoring in the workplace: A guide to its practical application to chemical exposure* HSG167 HSE Books 1997 ISBN 978 0 7176 1279 6

10 *Urine sampling for isocyanate exposure measurement* COSHH essentials sheet G408 HSE 2006 www.hse.gov.uk/pubns/guidance/g408.pdf

11 *Health surveillance for occupational asthma* COSHH essentials sheet G402 HSE 2006
www.hse.gov.uk/pubns/guidance/g402.pdf

12 *Motor vehicle repair: Good practice for SMART sprayers* WEB33 HSE 2007
www.hse.gov.uk/pubns/web33.pdf

13 *Manual handling. Manual Handling Operations Regulations 1992 (as amended). Guidance on Regulations* L23 (Third edition) HSE Books 2004
ISBN 978 0 7176 2823 0

14 BS AU 159f:1997 *Specification for repairs to tyres for motor vehicles used on the public highway* British Standards Institution

15 BS EN 471:2003 *High-visibility warning clothing for professional use. Test methods and requirements* British Standards Institution

16 PAS 43:2008 *Safe working of vehicle breakdown, recovery and removal operations: Management system specification* British Standards Institution

17 BS 7121–12:1999 *Safe use of cranes. Part 12: Recovery vehicles and equipment. Code of Practice* British Standards Institution

18 BS 7901:2002 *Specification for recovery vehicles and vehicle recovery equipment* British Standards Institution

19 *Safe recovery (and repair) of buses and coaches fitted with air suspension. Plant and Machinery Guidance Note* PM85 HSE 2007
www.hse.gov.uk/pubns/pm85.pdf

20 *Driving at work: Managing work-related road safety* Leaflet INDG382 HSE Books 2003 (single copy free or priced packs of 4 ISBN 978 0 7176 2740 0) www.hse.gov.uk/pubns/indg382.pdf

21 *Safe working with LPG-fuelled motor vehicles* Leaflet INDG387 HSE Books 2003 (single copy free or priced packs of 10 ISBN 978 0 7176 2755 4) www.hse.gov.uk/pubns/indg387.pdf

22 BS 7980:2003 *Vehicle lifts. Installation, maintenance, thorough examination and safe use. Code of practice* British Standards Institution

23 BS EN 1493:1999 *Vehicle lifts* British Standards Institution

24 *Safe use of lifting equipment. Lifting Operations and Lifting Equipment Regulations 1998. Approved Code of Practice and guidance* L113 HSE Books 1998 ISBN 978 0 7176 1628 2

25 *Safe use of work equipment. Provision and Use of Work Equipment Regulations 1998. Approved Code of Practice and guidance* L22 (Third edition) HSE Books 2008 ISBN 978 0 7176 6295 1

26 *Compressed air safety* HSG39 (Second edition) HSE Books 1998 ISBN 978 0 7176 1531 5

27 *Controlling noise at work. The Control of Noise at Work Regulations 2005. Guidance on Regulations* L108 (Second edition) HSE Books 2005 ISBN 978 0 7176 6164 0

28 *Hand-arm vibration. The Control of Vibration at Work Regulations 2005. Guidance on Regulations* L140 HSE Books 2005 ISBN 978 0 7176 6125 1

29 *Hand-arm vibration: Advice for employees* Pocket card INDG296(rev1) HSE Books 2005 (single copy free or priced packs of 25 ISBN 978 0 7176 6118 3) www.hse.gov.uk/pubns/indg296.pdf

30 *Dangerous substances and explosive atmospheres. Dangerous Substances and Explosive Atmospheres Regulations 2002. Approved Code of Practice and guidance* L138 HSE Books 2003 ISBN 978 0 7176 2203 0

31 *The Equipment and Protective Systems Intended for Use in Potentially Explosive Atmospheres Regulations* 1996 (as amended) SI 1996/192 The Stationery Office 1996

32 *Fire and explosion: How safe is your workplace? A short guide to the Dangerous Substances and Explosive Atmospheres Regulations* Leaflet INDG370 HSE Books 2002 (single copy free or priced packs of 5 ISBN 978 0 7176 2589 5) www.hse.gov.uk/pubns/indg370.pdf

33 *Safe working with flammable substances* Leaflet INDG227 HSE Books 1996 (single copy free or priced packs of 15 ISBN 978 0 7176 1154 6) www.hse.gov.uk/pubns/indg227.pdf

34 *Choosing a welding set? Make sure you can handle it* Leaflet INDG390(rev1) HSE Books 2009 (single copy free or priced packs of 10 ISBN 978 0 7176 6384 2) www.hse.gov.uk/pubns/indg390.pdf

35 *Safety in gas welding, cutting and similar processes* Leaflet INDG297 HSE Books 1999 (single copy free or priced packs of 10 ISBN 978 0 7176 2473 7) www.hse.gov.uk/pubns/indg297.pdf

36 *Hot work on small tanks and drums* Leaflet INDG314 HSE Books 2000 (single copy free or priced packs of 10 ISBN 978 0 7176 1766 1) www.hse.gov.uk/pubns/indg314.pdf

37 *Storage of dangerous substances. Dangerous Substances and Explosive Atmospheres Regulations 2002. Approved Code of Practice and guidance* L135 HSE Books 2003 ISBN 978 0 7176 2200 9

38 *Safe maintenance, repair and cleaning procedures. Dangerous Substances and Explosive Atmospheres Regulations 2002. Approved Code of Practice and guidance* L137 HSE Books 2003 ISBN 978 0 7176 2202 3

39 *The storage of flammable liquids in containers* HSG51 (Second edition) HSE Books 1998 ISBN 978 0 7176 1471 4

40 *Safe use and handling of flammable liquids* HSG140 HSE Books 1996 ISBN 978 0 7176 0967 3

41 *The storage of flammable liquids in tanks* HSG176 HSE Books 1998 ISBN 978 0 7176 1470 7

42 EN 175:1997 *Personal protection. Equipment for eye and face protection during welding and allied processes* British Standards Institution

43 EN 169:2002 *Personal eye protection. Filters for welding and related techniques* British Standards Institution

44   EN 379:2003 *Personal eye protection. Automatic welding filters* British Standards Institution

45   *Memorandum of guidance on the Electricity at Work Regulations 1989. Guidance on Regulations* HSR25 (Second edition) HSE Books 2007 ISBN 978 0 7176 6228 9

46   BS EN 60079 series *Electrical apparatus for explosive gas atmospheres* British Standards Institution

47   BS 7671:2008 *Requirements for Electrical Installations* British Standards Institution

48   *Guidance Note 3 to IEE Wiring Regulations BS7671. Inspection and Testing* Institution of Electrical Engineers 2002

49   BS EN 60309 series *Plugs, socket-outlets and couplers for industrial purposes* British Standards Institution

50   *Maintaining portable and transportable electrical equipment* HSG107 (Second edition) HSE Books 2004 ISBN 978 0 7176 2805 6

51   *Selection and use of electric handlamps* Plant and Machinery Guidance Note PM38 (Second edition) HSE 2007 www.hse.gov.uk/pubns/guidance/pm38.pdf

52   BS ISO 23273-3:2006 *Fuel cell road vehicles. Safety specifications. Protection of persons against electric shock* British Standards Institution

53   BS ISO 6469-3:2001 *Electric road vehicles. Safety specifications. Part 3: Protection of persons against electric hazards* British Standards Institution

54   BS EN 60529:1992 *Specification for degrees of protection provided by enclosures* British Standards Institution

55   *Electrical risks from steam/water pressure cleaners* Plant and Machinery Guidance Note PM29 (Second edition) HSE Books 1995 ISBN 978 0 7176 0813 3

56   *Do you use a steam/water pressure cleaner? You could be in for a shock!* Leaflet INDG68(rev) HSE Books 1997 (single copy free) www.hse.gov.uk/pubns/indg68.pdf

57   *The Work at Height Regulations 2005 (as amended): A brief guide* Leaflet INDG401(rev1) HSE Books 2007 (single copy free or priced packs of 10 ISBN 978 0 7176 6231 9) www.hse.gov.uk/pubns/indg401.pdf

58   *Workplace health, safety and welfare. Workplace (Health, Safety and Welfare) Regulations 1992. Approved Code of Practice* L24 HSE Books 1992 ISBN 978 0 7176 0413 5

59   *Work with display screen equipment. Health and Safety (Display Screen Equipment) Regulations 1992 as amended by the Health and Safety (Miscellaneous Amendments) Regulations 2002. Guidance on Regulations* L26 (Second edition) HSE Books 2003 ISBN 978 0 7176 2582 6

60   *A guide to the Reporting of Injuries, Diseases and Dangerous Occurrences Regulations 1995* L73 (Third edition) HSE Books 2008 ISBN 978 0 7176 6290 6

61   *Five steps to risk assessment* Leaflet INDG163(rev2) HSE Books 2006 (single copy free or priced packs of 10 ISBN 978 0 7176 6189 3) www.hse.gov.uk/pubns/indg163.pdf

62   *Basic advice on first aid at work* Leaflet INDG347(rev1) HSE Books 2006 (single copy free or priced packs of 20 ISBN 978 0 7176 6193 0) www.hse.gov.uk/pubns/indg347.pdf

63   *Accident book* BI 510 HSE Books 2003 ISBN 978 0 7176 2603 8

64   *Consulting employees on health and safety: A brief guide to the law* INDG232(rev1) HSE Books 2008 (single copy free or priced packs of 15 ISBN 978 0 7176 6312 5) www.hse.gov.uk/pubns/indg232.pdf

Further reading

Reducing ill health and accidents in motor vehicle repair Leaflet INDG356(rev1) HSE Books 2009 (single copies free or priced packs of 10 ISBN 978 0 7176 6376 7) www.hse.gov.uk/pubns/indg356.pdf

Safety in motor vehicle repair: Working with isocyanate paints Leaflet INDG388(rev1) HSE Books 2009 (single copies free or priced packs of 10 ISBN 978 0 7176 6381 1) www.hse.gov.uk/pubns/indg388.pdf

Further information

More advice can be found on HSE's motor vehicle repair website at: www.hse.gov.uk/mvr.

For information about health and safety ring HSE's Infoline Tel: 0845 345 0055 Fax: 0845 408 9566 Textphone: 0845 408 9577 e-mail: hse.infoline@ natbrit.com or write to HSE Information Services, Caerphilly Business Park, Caerphilly CF83 3GG.

HSE priced and free publications can be viewed online or ordered from www.hse.gov.uk or contact HSE Books, PO Box 1999, Sudbury, Suffolk CO10 2WA Tel: 01787 881165 Fax: 01787 313995 Website: http://books.hse.gov.uk (HSE priced publications are also available from bookshops).

British Standards can be obtained in PDF or hard copy formats from BSI: http://shop.bsigroup.com or by contacting BSI Customer Services for hard copies only Tel: 020 8996 9001 e-mail: cservices@bsigroup.com.

The Stationery Office publications are available from The Stationery Office, PO Box 29, Norwich NR3 1GN Tel: 0870 600 5522 Fax: 0870 600 5533 e-mail: customer.services@tso.co.uk Website: www.tso.co.uk (They are also available from bookshops.) Statutory Instruments can be viewed free of charge at www.opsi.gov.uk.

Printed and published by the Health and Safety Executive   C50   10/09